Finding Our Voices

Finding Our Voices

Women, Wisdom, and Faith

Patricia O'Connell Killen

A Crossroad Book
The Crossroad Publishing Company
New York

1997

The Crossroad Publishing Company
370 Lexington Avenue, New York, New York 10017

Cover art: *Elizabeth the Wonder-Worker*, icon by Kathleen O'Connell Sievers.

Unless otherwise noted, all scripture in this book is taken from the *New Revised Standard Version,* The New Oxford Annotated Bible with the Apocrypha: An Ecumenical Study Bible (New York: Oxford University Press, 1994).

Printed in the United States of America

Library of Congress Cataloging-in-Publication Data

Killen, Patricia O'Connell.
    Finding our voices : women, wisdom, and faith / Patricia O'Connell Killen.
        p.   cm.
    "A Crossroad book."
    Includes bibliographical references.
    ISBN 0-8245-1610-9 (pbk.)
    1. Catholic women—Religious life.   2. Women in the Catholic Church.   3. Christian women—Religious life.   4. Women in Christianity.   I. Title.
BX2353.K55   1997
277.3'082'082—dc21   97-37544
                                                                        CIP

For
Florence O'Connell, Sylvia Peters
Roberta Hutton, Jane Rinehart, Mary Sharon Riley, r.c.
Mother, aunt, teachers, friends—
women who have shown me wisdom

Contents

Acknowledgments   ix

Preface   xi

1. A Glimpse into Wise Faith   1

2. Promise, Perils, and Ambiguity   10

3. Listening to Our Longings   23

4. Embracing Frustrated Longing: A Woman's Act
    of Faith   41

5. The Power of Voice   59

6. Finding a Voice, Discovering Faith:
    Becoming a Public Person   84

7. Voice as Faith: Women's Path   99

8. Walking Wisdom's Path   113

Notes   131

Acknowledgments

Sometimes ideas and insights are awakened in us through the beckoning call of others. When their call resonates with passion in our own depth, surprising things emerge, creative projects we would never have imagined for ourselves. That is how this book came to be.

The beckoning call sounded in a series of invitations over the past five years to lecture, preach, lead retreats, facilitate women's groups, give workshops, and deliver a parish mission. In all of these invitations I was asked to focus on the experience of women of faith, past and present. To those who invited me, to those who listened, and to those who participated, I am grateful. Invitations came from the Cenacle, Wayzata, Minnesota; the Women Becoming Lecture Series sponsored by the Minneapolis League of Catholic Women; St. Joseph's Catholic Church, Seattle, Washington; St. Leo Catholic Church, Tacoma, Washington; University Women's Club of Washington, Seattle, Washington; Tacoma Deanery, Archdiocese of Seattle; Diocese of Joliet, Joliet, Illinois; Russell County Cluster, Women of the Evangelical Lutheran Church of America, Great Falls, Montana; Grace Lutheran Church, Des Moines, Washington; Creator Lutheran Church, Lake Tapps, Washington; Priory Spirituality Center, St. Placid's Priory, Lacey, Washington; National Parish Coordinators and Directors of Religious Education of the National Catholic Education Association; and Ascension Parish, Oak Park, Illinois.

I want to express my appreciation as well to the scores of women without whose scholarship in biblical studies, history, and theology over the past thirty-five years this book would not be possible. Their research has retrieved foremothers in faith from oblivion. Making them visible again, they have made contemporary women of faith more visible to themselves. Their scholarship raises critical questions about the consequences for women and for our understanding of God of pervasive androcentrism and patriarchy in church and society. Finally, their work encourages their students, companions, sisters, spouses, and friends to imagine and struggle for a world and church in which women are understood to be fully in the image of God.

Conversations with friends have been vital to the development of this book. I am particularly grateful to Mary Kaye Cisek, Myrel Cook, Madeline Duntley, Sherry Fisher, C. J. Franklin, the late Ann Graff, Nancy Howell, Judy Logue, Heidi McCormick, Mary Sharon Riley, Jane Rinehart, Kathleen O'Connell Sievers, Kathleen Sullivan-Stewart, and Felicia Wolf for their willingness to listen and to engage with me the difficult issues that are part of being women in church and society today. My sister, Kathleen O'Connell Sievers, introduced me to her icon of Elizabeth the Wonder-Worker during one of our conversations. I am grateful to her for allowing me to include the icon in this book.

Friends whom I trust to be good and honest critics read earlier drafts of the manuscript and provided me with pointed challenges and valuable suggestions. Thank you, Reverend Mary Jane Francis, Peter Gilmour, Judy Logue, Travis Pardo, Felicia Wolf, O.S.F., and Richard Woods, O.P. The book is far stronger for your perceptive insights.

The last stages of bringing a book to life can be especially difficult. The work was made easier for me by the Generalate Community, Religious of the Cenacle, in Rome, Italy. The gracious hospitality and solitude that they provided me in November of 1996 made it possible to complete this work. My colleague, Peter Glimour, of the Institute of Pastoral Studies, Loyola University, also supported the project by extending me the use of his Camp Lake retreat for writing.

My husband, David Killen, exhibited great patience during the months that I was preoccupied with this project. At crucial moments he also eased my condition as writer by contributing his expertise with the computer. For this and for more than can be said, I am grateful.

My editor at The Crossroad Publishing Company, Lynn Schmitt Quinn, has been unwavering in her enthusiasm and support for this project from its earliest inception. With patience, incisive editorial guidance, and good humor she has been midwife to the creative process.

Finally, to all those who contributed to this project whose names remain unspoken, thank you.

Preface

This book emerged from a series of invitations to speak about historical and contemporary women in the Christian tradition. Those lectures and retreats focused primarily on how these women lived creatively as women of faith in a world and in churches that often diminished them. In preparing my presentations I drew on my knowledge as a historian of Christianity, especially Christianity in the United States, and on my experience as a Catholic Christian woman whose journey has taken her from a rural, ethnic subculture to the life of the academy. Professionally and personally, then, I am interested in how Christian women in differing social, cultural contexts draw on their religious heritage as they seek God, criticize their worlds, and face new challenges with courage and creativity.

When I began giving my presentations I was surprised by the intensity of the response from the women in my audiences. They valued learning about their foremothers in faith. Even more, they relished the approaches that I suggested for drawing on their religious heritage as a resource for their ordinary lives. The image of "journey to voice as a journey to wise faith" delighted them most. Thinking about their lives as a journey to faithful voice and wisdom opened spaces of possibility for them. This book was written for the women I encountered in my audiences who requested that I "write down" what I said, and for countless other women like them—women of faith who long for more.

—Patricia O'Connell Killen

1

A Glimpse into Wise Faith

~~❧~~

Faith, Disillusionment, and Hunger for God

On a rainy February evening I sat with fifteen women in the rectory library at a local parish. It was the first of three sessions the group had invited me to facilitate. They wanted to reflect on the relationship between their Catholic Christian heritage and their lives as women. Though I had not met the women before, I knew that together we could weave a litany of occasions in our lives when we experienced a dark side to our Christian heritage, mostly through its leadership or teachings, but also through the words or actions of other Christians, as hurtful, harmful, dumb, obscure, opaque, or irrelevant to us as women. Still, we were there in the parish library, gathered around the table.

"Why have you come this evening?" I asked the women. "Because I feel like I'm standing by a river, dying of thirst," answered a newcomer to the group. The rest of us sat quietly, soaking in the truthfulness of her response. We all knew what she meant. Her words evoked silence from us because they gave voice to the deep, often frustrated, but still hope-filled longing that the rest of us shared: the longing to be nourished by our Christian heritage on our journeys to God, a longing coupled with the painful realization that often we are not.

The woman's image evoked a powerful response because it expressed so well a profoundly disturbing, widespread, and significant experience for contemporary women of faith: simultaneously awakening to the intensity of our longing for God and to our disappointment and disillusionment with our religious heritage as we admit the ways it has discounted, damaged, and refused to support us on our journeys to God. This dual awakening is a particularly painful and challenging moment in any woman's life. It engenders a rush of questions that Christian women are asking in myriad ways: Can my religious heritage carry life-giving power for me instead of death, bring me delight instead of diminishment? Can my religious heritage ground serious critique of myself, my society, and my denominational tradition; and, at the same time, inspire my imagination so that I can live creatively and faithfully? Does my religious tradition empower or encumber genuine freedom of action in me? And in some ways the most vexing question of all: Should I stay or leave?

The newcomer articulated her intense longing for God and her disillusionment with her tradition in an image: She was "standing by a river dying of thirst." I have heard the experience and its questions expressed in many images and direct statements by women from all over the world through two decades in courses, workshops, and retreats. The experience and its questions are my companions as well.

In my own religious journey I live the tension that simultaneously hungering for God and being disillusioned with a religious heritage creates. I have known hurt and abuse at the hands of my church, its designated leaders, and its traditional teachings—all of which have, at times, denied my dignity and worth as a female human person. I have known profound experiences of healing and empowerment that have come through Catholic Christianity's theological and spiritual teachings and its ritual and sacramental practices. How to reconcile these divergent experiences? My church and its traditions unquestionably are guilty of the sin of sexism. My church and its traditions also have mediated God's life to me. To deny either of these statements would be dishonest. To face them both raises complicated issues of intellectual honesty, personal integrity, and faithfulness to God that are not easily resolved.

Facing both the life-giving and the death-dealing dimensions of my Catholic Christian heritage is, however, the path to which I have found myself called on the journey of faith. Only by walking this path will I touch the answer to the spiritual question that underlies the other questions women ask when they awaken to their hunger for God and their disillusionment with their Christian heritage: What is the transforming gift of this insight, an insight that begins so often in heartbreaking experiences of disillusionment?

I do not ask this question lightly. The pain of women in the church today is real. So too is their disillusionment and discouragement.[1] Conversations with friends in parishes where new pastors summarily dismiss liturgy committees and professional staff, both paid and volunteer, are difficult and all too frequent for me. Female college students who tell me that the Mass has no meaning for them and that they will "go crazy" if they hear God referred to as "he" one more time file into my university office with regularity. The stories of all these women lead me to reflect on my integrity as a Catholic Christian woman and my relationship to my religious tradition. I cannot deny that I am fed by a tradition that also is used to justify oppression and abuse, that I belong to an institution that is in part destructive. This growing body of experience challenges my intellectual and spiritual integrity.

Yet, what I have come to know through taking the path of facing both the life-giving and the death-dealing dimensions of my Catholic Christian heritage is that my tradition contains liberating truth deeper and more powerful than the androcentrism and patriarchy of my church. I have come to believe that women of faith have found this liberating truth by drawing on two resources as they journeyed in faith: their Christian heritage and their own lived experience of God. Drawing on both, women have known that though they were first in faith from the Annunciation to the Empty Tomb, they have faced oppression within the Christian community because they are women. From the beginning, women's faith has called them to resistance, to biting criticism, and to a trust in their religious heritage so deep that they persist in hope, in the obstinate demand that their hunger for God be fed. Women's faith—their relationships with God—invites them to connect to the deep resources of a decidedly sinful Christian tradition and community, flawed and frail because it is profoundly human, even as Jesus' spirit continues to be present there. This embodied faith is at once critical and hopeful, resistant and joyful. It funds women's confidence that there is something for them in the Christian heritage even when church leaders say there is not. It grounds women's belief that the tradition offers them insight and affirmation on the journey to God that clerical interpreters and keepers of the tradition cannot finally obscure. This faith has supported women for generations to be nourished by the Christian tradition, even as they have endured oppression perpetrated in the name of the gospel. This is wise faith—a faith that allows women to hold themselves and their tradition gently, but to take both seriously, because of what is at stake and because of their trust in God. Wise faith is the surprising, unsettling gift that may begin to develop when a woman recognizes that her Christian heritage brings her death as well as life.

I have chosen to name this gift *wise faith. Wise* is grounded in the Wisdom tradition of Jewish Scripture, a tradition on which the earliest followers of Jesus drew to interpret the meaning of his life, death, and resurrection.[2] Wise faith roots women in the resources of their tradition, but in a part of the tradition that propels them to pay attention to their own processes of development as human persons; for Wisdom literature focuses attention on the well-being of humans in their concrete and particular social, cultural, and religious situations.[3] *Faith* refers to a particular individual's relationship of trust with God. Any kind of faith—wise or otherwise—cannot be conceived separately from growth in awareness and agency. Hence, current insights into women's social, psychological, and spiritual development also provide resources for understanding the promise and perils to women's faith as they face the dual reality of their Christian tradition.

Wise faith, then, embodies dimensions of wisdom widely recognized by religious and humanistic traditions. It invites us to consider the multiple dynamics of spiritual, psychological, and social development in women as they confront simultaneously their intense desire for God and their disillusionment with their religious heritage. Wise faith beckons women to an alternative standpoint from which to consider their relationship to themselves, their Christian tradition, and their society. It offers a map, so to speak, that might guide contemporary Christian women through the experience of simultaneous desire and disillusionment.

Fully developed, wise faith can ground women creatively in relation to their religious heritage and their own experience. It reflects an honest and accurate but not reviling or loathing relationship to one's own humanity and one's companions in creation. It surprises in its capacity to perceive dimensions of reality and relational patterns within it that others do not see. It grows with a gentle capacity to feel and to think, and to speak what one feels and thinks. It funds commitment to visions and values beyond oneself, but does not turn values into idols. It is a faith that is embodied in deliberate actions aimed toward self, others, and world to restore harmonious relations and richer existence. Wise faith opens a range of freedom of action, delight, and creativity.[4] This is not the faith of little girls or of male-defined women. It is the faith of sturdy, delighted, honest, compassionate women. It is the faith that allows women to "drink from the river."

Wise faith is what the newcomer was seeking when she came that night to the parish library, feeling that she was "standing by a river, dying of thirst." I believe it is what most women who remain within Christian denominations seek: a faith that creatively confronts the death-dealing and the life-giving dimensions of our Christian heritage, that finds healthy and nurturing ways to reconceive and relate to that tradition, and that uncovers possibilities for fuller life.

Such faith does not come to a woman as an intellectual concept to be possessed, however, or as a self-willed state of autonomous freedom. Rather, wise faith comes finally as gift, a surprising, unsettling gift that a woman receives as she makes the journey into her life.

The Journey Toward Wise Faith

The journey toward wise faith changes a woman. Beginning this journey means entering a process of ongoing transformation in which her relationship to herself and her religious heritage is recast. As a woman progresses along this journey she may find herself gradually becoming capable of both criticism and creativity, more honest about reality, and more hopeful about possibilities that can arise even from death. On the journey toward wise faith a woman may learn how to be constructively nourished by her religious heritage even as she actively resists the harm her Christian community might inflict on her through teaching or practice.

If as contemporary women of faith we are to move through our dual awakening—longing for God and disillusionment with our religious traditions—to a place of nourishment in our faith journeys, then we must undertake the journey toward wise faith. To take this path we will need to attend more closely to our own experiences of God, to our relationships to our Christian tradition, and to the experiences of our foremothers in faith. In community with them and with our sisters in faith today we will find support and resist self-deception as we move through our experience of simultaneous desire and disillusionment. In community with them we begin to discover that ambiguity has always been the context within which women have journeyed toward God.

When we attend to their journeys we may discover important things about our foremothers; their lives contained much more than we have been told or been willing to see. Their lives consisted of more than obedience to the authority of the church and willingness to extend themselves in service to the world. These women were not always obedient. Neither did their lives consist of nothing but "doormat" service. They found ways to be self-fulfilled in both their resistance and their compliance. These women knew something of God and something of what it means to be human beings. Many knew courage and hope and faith deeper than the abuses they often endured at the hands of the church. They were more rounded, fuller, more human characters than we might imagine. They were holy and wise women with a capacity to resist oppression, to live within a damaged and damaging Christian community and still to be able to draw on its resources, to create for themselves zones of freedom in which they could know joy in God.[5] If we begin to see our foremothers in this way, we may see new dimensions of our own experience. As we look at our own and our foremothers' journeys in faith, we begin to put words to our experiences, to trust their integrity despite what those with institutional power say to us. Perhaps we can come to know our flawed and frail Christian heritage as a life-giving resource for our lives in a new way.

How to make this journey toward wise faith? Two things are required. First, we must walk into our lives and notice, feel, and reflect on all of our experiences. This self-reflection requires an honest facing of the life-giving and the death-dealing elements in our relationship to our religious heritage. This search requires us to take ourselves seriously, to address, listen to, and hear ourselves individually and corporately as women with all the diversity of our experiences. Then we must utter what we know. *We must find our own voices.* Second, we must turn to our mothers and foremothers and see their humanity and their faith in its own terms. They are our forbearers. They are our companions. Their stories provide us an alternative context for exploring and defining our reality, a context that stands in critical contrast to the male-defined reality provided by the institutional church. Dimensions of our mothers' stories show us things we did not know about our own. Reflection on our own experiences allows us to notice things not seen in their stories. Understanding and giving voice to our own and our mothers' experiences as women of faith—especially experiences of realizing the dual quality of our Christian heritage as death-dealing and life-giving—is the process that can lead us toward wisdom.

Walking into our own experience and paying attention to our mothers' stories are not easy. These acts require considerable personal courage. We must walk through experiences of awakening to the longing for God, through frustration and disillusionment with the institution that should have helped satisfy that longing and so often has not. Taking these steps, we may find ourselves at the place of interdependent power and perception where our mothers both criticized and drew upon the tradition that they never experienced as completely for them. Standing with them, we must ask if this is a place we too can occupy. We must confront the overwhelmingly male character of designated leadership in the church, the systematic demeaning of women in the tradition of Catholic theology and practice, and a world intent on denying the integrity of women's voices, work, and even our very selves. We must learn to notice in our foremothers' words and stories and lives moments of freedom, joy, creative imagination, and intimacy with God also mediated through the resources of this same church and tradition, and ask honestly if we can know the same. We must identify our foremothers' strategies for faithful living; empathize with their joy and intimacy with God; share their sense of limits, loss, and sorrow; and return to our own unique spiritual and life journeys. Then we must choose our own lives, wherever they take us, choosing in hope that having learned from our mothers we will not repeat a past that demeans and destroys us.

An Invitation to Make the Journey Toward Wise Faith

This book invites you, the reader, to reflect on your journey toward wise faith. This journey will ask you to consider the vision of Wisdom as God's Spirit active in our midst from the biblical heritage. It requires you to contemplate the obstacles to making the journey that are put forward by society, self, and church. It will take you into your own experiences of hungering for God and disillusionment with your Christian heritage and into the lives of your foremothers in faith. The journey asks you to embrace your longing for God and to begin to notice your own voice of faith as a possible path into a newly renegotiated relationship to the Christian heritage. The journey toward wise faith invites you to move more deeply into the Christian heritage so that it can nurture constructive criticism and generate imagination for creative action in your life. It asks you to try on new ways of perceiving yourself, your faith, and your struggles with the church. After you have done so, you may answer for yourself—Can simultaneous desire for God and disillusionment with my religious tradition be a source of gift for me, the beginnings of wise faith?

The journey to wise faith is not an easy journey, but it is one that the church and the world need women to walk, as much as we ourselves need to walk it. As women we must learn to speak our faithful wisdom as a way to counter all those voices and institutions that discount, diminish, and violate us. We need to learn how to speak our faithful wisdom in order to make sure that our mothers and aunts and female neighbors who embodied faith for us and nurtured faith in us will not be forgotten. We need to learn how to speak our faithful wisdom as a way to teach our daughters that they too have dignity and are made in the image of God. As women we need to speak our faithful wisdom so that we may learn to love ourselves as God loves us, to praise God in our own voices, to bring healing to the planet, and to bring justice to the church.

Pause for Reflection

1. Think about your own journey of life and faith so far. Identify times when you were aware of your longing for God. Identify times when you were disillusioned with your Christian heritage or church community. Describe these experiences.

2. When you long for God and are disillusioned with your Christian heritage or church community, what questions do you ask?

3. *In what specific ways have you known your religious heritage to be death-dealing and life-giving? If you have not known it both ways, how have you seen it be both for other women?*

4. *What attracts you about the journey toward wise faith?*

2

Promise, Perils, and Ambiguity

తావ

The Context of Women's Journeys Toward Wise Faith

When we find ourselves "standing by a river, dying of thirst," simultaneously filled with longing for God and disillusionment with our religious heritage, we are bidden to undertake a journey. This journey beckons us toward wise faith. But we do not make the journey in a vacuum. We make it within the context of our lives, a context of both promise and peril. The promise comes from our Christian heritage and the vision it offers for fuller life. The peril arises from the obstacles a woman faces from herself, her world, and her church when she undertakes the journey to wise faith. Promise and peril create an ambiguous context for a woman's journey toward wise faith. But ambiguity itself can become a gift.

Scriptural Roots of Wise Faith

Wisdom is a complex image for God and God's Spirit among human beings in the Jewish and Christian Scriptures.[1] Associated intimately with God's Spirit, Wisdom is hard to contain. Wisdom is present in particular persons, teachings, actions, or decisions as a quality that attends them. It cannot be controlled, forced, willed, predicted, or produced by logical formula because it is God's Spirit present and active in the thick of historical existence. While we may desire Wisdom, we also fear it, because Wisdom plays; it subverts and inverts our worlds, our beliefs, our plans, constantly calling us to truer and fuller life.

Both Jewish and Christian Scriptures identify wise people as those who are in touch with God's Spirit among human beings. They discern the workings of God's Spirit in concrete situations and in the sweep of historical events. Wise people fascinate and sometimes frighten us because they grasp how to live life in congruence with the deepest reality. They have learned how to be patient and to sort out in the situations of daily life what brings life and what does not. A discerning quality characterizes their reflection and interaction.[2] They do not judge quickly, are more likely to question than to pontificate, and are more likely to be amused than annoyed by the small irritations of life.

In scripture and in our own time, wise people understand that the focus of Wisdom (God's Spirit) is on life here and now, in history. Wisdom was with God at creation and continues to be in creation and in created beings. Wisdom's goal is rich life for all individuals and communities. This richness is interior and exterior, individual and social, physical and spiritual, historical and self-transcending. More than any of the other thematic threads in the biblical material, Wisdom rejects deferring fulfillment of individual or communal life to some future, eternal place.[3]

Wisdom pushes us to understand ourselves within the larger context of God's creation. It calls us to discern how we need to act to be most fully who we are called to be. Wisdom teaches what gives life and what does not. It focuses on the patterns of consequences to actions. For example, the sayings in Proverbs may seem calculated to advance self-interest: "A gracious woman gets honor, but she who hates virtue is covered with shame" (Prv 11:16). But at a deeper level such pragmatic teachings convey Wisdom's claims about the structures of reality. So, Proverbs 11:16 is not just about how a woman creates a good life for herself; it also makes a claim against the contrary view that would say a woman who is gracious leaves herself open to others' taking advantage of her.[4]

Wisdom's concerns lead to a distinctive understanding and practice of authority, one quite different from that practiced in the church today. Wisdom does not justify its claims by appeal to scripture, doctrine, role, office, or human or divine government. The authority of Wisdom's claims rests in the statements themselves. They are invitations to try living life in a particular way and to see the result. The authority of a teaching is determined by its fruit as found in the common experience of the community.[5] Wisdom's way of conceiving authority, then, authorizes the critique of any system that concentrates power in the hands of a few.

Wisdom accents the incarnational and the creative. It trusts humans to be able to discern the basic order of the cosmos and live creatively according to this order. Human creativity brings fullness of life for all of creation. Moral failure, from Wisdom's perspective, is not the result of resistance to an authoritative teacher or text but unwillingness to read the signs of the times and to discern the processes that make for life and for death for ourselves and for our communities. From Wisdom's perspective, our choices matter. Whether we become discerning persons matters. Whether we become the kinds of persons who can understand and value themselves within the larger context of God's creative process matters.[6]

The Jewish religious tradition has a long line of teachers of Wisdom, individuals whose capacities for discernment and discrimination about the movement of God's Spirit in the world made them models for others of how to live and how to discern. Teachers of wisdom have well-developed capacities to discern the dimensions and depths of reality. These individuals teach in a way that invites others to discern the movements of God in the day-in and day-out of living. "Teacher of Wisdom" was one of the earliest concepts that the followers of Jesus turned to as they began to interpret the fuller meaning of his life in light of the Resurrection.[7]

Jewish teachers of Wisdom taught about two kinds of wisdom: conventional and subversive. Conventional wisdom consists of all the teachings and practices that reinforce current reality, that locate people's security and worth in their current roles or possessions. Conventional wisdom is what everybody already knows. It is the set of principles and ideological agreements that shore up our reality. Conventional wisdom provides guidance about how to live, guidance based in the values of the dominant or most powerful people in a culture. It structures life according to a system of rigid rewards and punishments, using fear to achieve compliance.

It creates multiple boundaries, hierarchies, and classes. It promotes a life of anxious striving in which an individual's value depends upon his or her accomplishments and possessions.[8]

The other kind of wisdom is an alternative or subversive wisdom, a wisdom that sees the incompleteness of a particular individual, corporate, or institutional choice and invites hearers to notice the inadequacy and to choose a larger, richer, more inclusive vision of life. Alternative wisdom invites this choice, ironically, by teaching a narrower way. It invites people to see reality differently and to live a different reality. Teachers of alternative wisdom do not appeal to law but to the imagination of their hearers. They seek to create contexts for insight, imaginative spaces where people, having looked at life through new eyes, might be able to live a fuller, richer life.[9]

Jesus of Nazareth was a teacher of subversive or alternative wisdom. Through his aphorisms and parables he invited his listeners into a relationship with God different from that defined by the purity codes of his day. Jesus' aphorisms and parables were not directed to people's wills. In this type of teaching he did not say, "Do this." Rather, he said, "Consider seeing it [reality, God, or a representative human situation] this way."[10]

Jesus used an invitational mode of teaching. He relied on the authority of Wisdom: the authenticity of the teaching itself when experienced in daily living.[11] In the tradition of the great Wisdom teachers, Jesus did not appeal to office or to prior authoritative tradition. He appealed to the effective power of the tradition's teachings in people's lives. Not "because I said so" but "live it and see" characterized his way of teaching. This way offers a passionate invitation to people to experience and live fuller lives, but it leaves them free, eschewing coercion or manipulation as strategies for gaining their compliance.

Jesus' alternative wisdom suggested that the response to the transitory nature of life need not be clinging and scarcity but gratitude and gracious enjoyment. Jesus' alternative wisdom did not focus on God as the strict lawgiver but as the womb-like lover of creation.[12] Jesus invited people along a narrow path, a path focused increasingly on God and not on the values and orientations of conventional wisdom.[13]

In both the Jewish and Christian traditions, Wisdom offers an alternative to conventional ways of viewing and living life. It subverts seemingly solid and divinely sanctioned authorities and institutions, resting on no appeal to authority other than the authenticity of its claims lived out in the day-to-day experiences of people. Wisdom invites us to discernment, an invitation that entails developing our perceptions, our voice, and our faith. The consequences of discernment are speech and action for life and against death as those forces play out in the myriad particular situations of our individual and corporate lives.

Obstacles on the Journey to Wise Faith

The journey toward wise faith is demanding of us personally. The promise for fuller, richer life for women in relationship to all of creation can be fulfilled only if we cooperate with God's Spirit in our midst. That cooperation requires a particular way of being in the world, one that the Wisdom literature of scripture outlines. Learning to practice that way of being is not easy. It is made more difficult by the lack of support and even active resistance on the part of our religious and secular worlds. Encountering resistance is one of the perils of the journey toward wise faith. Resistance arises from the profoundly androcentric and patriarchal nature of those worlds.

An androcentric world is male-centered. It assumes: 1) that male and human are the same thing; 2) that because they are identical "the generic masculine habit of thought, language, and research is adequate" to understanding human beings; and, 3) that "when women, per se, are considered, . . . they are discussed as an object, exterior to mankind, needing to be explained and fitted into one's worldview," like "trees" or "unicorns." In an androcentric world, then, women are basically marginal.[14] What matters in an androcentric world is what men want, do, and value. Women's activities and values are not considered important. They are secondary at best.

Patriarchy is the social order that grows out of an androcentric world view. It comprises the cultural and social systems of beliefs, institutions, and practices that keep men the center of attention and reality, keep power and resources concentrated in men's hands, and justify the discounting and devaluing of women.[15]

Androcentrism and patriarchy create serious obstacles to women's journeys in faith. One is the invisibility of women: to men, to themselves, and to each other. Our foremothers' stories are seldom part of our formation in faith. Women in the history of Christianity are mostly invisible due to the tradition's pervasive patriarchy and androcentrism. Mary Jo Weaver provides a pointed example of this invisibility in *New Catholic Women,* where she reports that of the sixty photographs in *Catholics in America 1776–1976,* thirty are of men and seven are of women. The remaining twenty-three are of buildings or political cartoons, with buildings outnumbering women two to one.[16] Lest we think the gap results only from old social practices governing photography, consider standard histories of American Catholicism such as James Hennessey's *American Catholics* or Jay Dolan's *The American Catholic Experience.* One finds perhaps ten pages on women in American Catholic history in books of four hundred pages.[17] The examples can be multiplied for virtually any Christian denomination in the United States.

Women's faith or actions are acknowledged in denominational histories or popular teaching, primarily in ways that show them as helpers to male authorities in the church. Women's self-directed activities are not considered important enough to mention. For example, altar societies in Catholic parishes are recognized for maintaining the church building and on occasion providing badly needed funds for the parish, and women's religious communities are recognized for providing badly needed educational services at low cost. Efforts to make visible women's more creative and enterprising roles in Christian denominations and the Christian theological tradition often are considered suspect, labeled dangerously subversive, derided as "radical feminism," or dismissed as bad or irrelevant scholarship.[18]

The absence and the distortion of women's lives and experiences in Christian history and theology hinder women's faith journeys. *When women grow up in a church and society where women are invisible, they become invisible to themselves.* Contemporary women struggle with this invisibility. First, we often do not notice or take seriously our own experiences, thoughts, and feelings. We have absorbed the androcentric and patriarchal assumption of our world that women are unimportant. So we devalue ourselves and make decisions about our time and resources detrimental to our own health and creative projects. Equally problematic, if we do begin to notice and describe our own experience, we are inclined to use concepts and frameworks borrowed from men's experience because it is the normative discourse for conceiving and judging ourselves. So, we criticize ourselves for not exercising leadership as men do, or for noticing so many dimensions of a situation that we fail to develop quick solutions to problems. Such thinking distorts our experience further and undercuts our capacity to make insightful judgments about it. When women do take steps to describe their experiences of God in their own terms and when they challenge the patriarchal status quo in religious institutions, they encounter fierce opposition.[19]

Besides grappling with the invisibility and distortion of women created by an androcentric Christian tradition and with active resistance to women defining their own religious experience and constructing theology from it, we also must overcome the "presentist" bias of our culture. This bias leads us to perceive and judge everything by the standards and values of our own day and to deny value in the distinctive cultures of the past. We need to be attuned to our foremothers of faith as people of their own times and cultures. They spoke and acted in ways that at first may offend late-twentieth-century sensibilities. We can be tempted to dismiss them again, because we read them through standards of equity, freedom, or women's rights forged in the twentieth century. To understand our foremothers in faith we need to approach them with a critical historical consciousness, willing at times to suspend our own world view in order to enter theirs as empathetically as possible. Even what disturbs or angers us about these women potentially offers insight into our own lives.

If our religious worlds are less than supportive of the tasks of entering reflectively into women's experience and learning from our foremothers in faith, so too is the larger culture. Androcentrism and patriarchy permeate our world, with serious negative consequences for both men and women. Women earn significantly less than men; hold fewer positions of power and influence in business, government, the arts, health care, and education; are more subject to domestic violence; have their health concerns taken less seriously by physicians; suffer more severe age discrimination; and, along with their children, are disproportionately represented among the poor in the United States. The situation for women is even more dire in many other countries around the globe.[20]

Androcentrism and patriarchy profoundly shape the context within which women make their lives. By choice or circumstance women focus their energies mainly on survival, spouses, and children. What sense of self and creative projects women achieve in their own terms often emerge in the margins, around the edges of others' lives. While women's improvisational strategies are original and the fruits of their creativity are significant, the fact that they do their work and stitch their lives around the periphery leads them to discount themselves and their writing, art, community organizing, or whatever else they have done.[21] When women do begin to take themselves seriously, they face in myriad ways the opposition of a church and a world that do not want to change. That social and institutional resistance often feeds a woman's sense that she is at an impasse, with no way to move.[22]

Walking into our own experience and reflecting on it leads us to notice the realities of androcentrism and patriarchy and their consequences in women's lives. Doing so can be painful enough on its own terms. It is made more so by a culture that teaches us to despise limits and weakness, our own or anyone else's. But we cannot deny the truth of our own contexts if we are to reflect honestly.

Saying "Yes" to the Search for Wise Faith

Our religious heritage offers us as women a vision and promise for full life. This promise is captured in the theme of wisdom as conveyed in the Wisdom literature and in Jesus. Yet patriarchal and androcentric, our church and our world present obstacles to us as women as we seek to embody the vision of rich and full life for ourselves and for all of creation for which Wisdom calls. Such is the ambiguity of our situation as contemporary Christian women.

Despite the challenges posed by our religious and secular worlds, despite the courage that reflecting on our experience and learning from our foremothers in faith requires, there is no other way to God for us. *Our lives are our spiritual path.* We cannot avoid them and grow in faith. The ambiguity and oppressiveness of our contexts as women in church and in society, and for many of us dislocated relationships to particular Christian denominations or traditions, are the stuff of our spiritual path. We do not get to God, grow in faith, or become wise, if we will not walk this path. There is no other way to find our own faithful voices.

Ambiguity as Resource: Listening to Our Foremothers

Having faced the androcentrism of our church and world, our foremothers become even more important to us as resources. As we begin to understand them on their own terms, we come to realize that we share much with them. From very early in the history of Christianity women found themselves being shut out from and marginalized by the leadership of the community. From very early in the history of Christianity women found their experiences of the Risen Lord ignored or discounted. From very early in the history of Christianity women have known the double consciousness of longing for God and being crippled by teachings that, as women, they were not worthy to have that longing satisfied. Yet, women remained in the church, knew God's love intimately, and made their contributions to the Kingdom of God in our midst. They knew that God will fill us, whatever the obstacles. They knew that their longing for God and God's longing for them could not be denied.

The situation of women in Christianity, at least from the time of the earliest written documents, has been nothing if not ambiguous. Ambiguous situations defined the context of our foremothers' faith and define the context of our own. Engaging the ambiguity of our context—coming to know it as a place of both possibility and peril—is one step on the path toward wise faith.

Ambiguity's Power: Elizabeth the Wonder-Worker

Ambiguity in relationship to our religious heritage is both intimidating and inviting: intimidating because so much is unknown; inviting because the situation and its boundaries have not been defined firmly and so space for new possibilities and insights remains. The story of a fifth-century saint helps to illustrate.[23]

In the fifth century a female child was born to a family somewhere in the northeastern section of the Mediterranean world. They named her Elizabeth. She became a very learned young woman. When her parents died she gave away her possessions and entered a convent. Elizabeth was an ascetic, known for fasting, going barefoot, wearing the same garment repeatedly, and for her prayerfulness. Eventually she became abbess.

The emperor, Leo I, gave Elizabeth's convent a piece of land, ostensibly as an expression of respect for Elizabeth. But the land was inhabited by a large, fierce dragon. The dragon made the townspeople so afraid that they would not go out of the town.

Elizabeth went to the dragon's cave alone, carrying only a cross. She commanded the beast, "Come out!" After making the sign of the cross over the dragon, she grabbed it by the head, spit on it, and trampled it with her bare feet. Thus the new convent could be built and the townspeople could go out safely. Elizabeth became Elizabeth the Wonder-Worker.

Elizabeth is one of our foremothers, and we women of the Western Christian tradition in a time sixteen-hundred years distant from hers need to claim her. Her icon, which appears on the cover, exudes the ambiguities and possibilities of her situation in relation to church and world.

The icon is full of powerful images: a woman standing barefoot atop a dragon; a woman alone; a woman with her back to the dark cave; a woman holding a cross in her right hand with her left hand in the position of blessing; a woman foregrounded in wilderness with dragon, deep cave, and thorn bushes; a woman backgrounded by city, church, monastery, mountains, or a melange of all of them. The images communicate ambiguous claims about the source of Elizabeth's power—is it from the church or from God?; about the extent of the church's and city's power—they are in the background; and about the relationship between life and death—is the dark cave a place of birth or a tomb? Is Elizabeth a resurrected Christ or a newly born goddess?

The icon exudes a blurring and crossing of boundaries and a woman full of potency. Elizabeth conquers the dragon by carrying the cross of Christ after an emperor had failed to conquer it. Elizabeth's power resides in her own deep relationship to the sacred, not in the institutional power of the church. She takes possession of land given but not controlled by the emperor, understood as a leader of the institutional church in Eastern

Christianity. What kind of statement is the story making about the power of church or state when an emperor gives what he does not fully possess? and when a woman has the power to possess what the emperor cannot? Elizabeth is an abbess, and so she locates herself within the church, but is she *of* it? What is the status of a monastery that cannot be built until a woman exercises her power? Just how connected to the church is Elizabeth?

The story of Elizabeth suggests that she was in touch with power not available to the emperor or the men of the town. She slayed the dragon and was not afraid. Because of her the townspeople were freed to go out of the town and to make journeys. Elizabeth is in touch with a power that can deconstruct entire societies built on fear.

Elizabeth both fits and does not fit the conventions of her day. She is cut loose in some way from the world that she not only inhabits but in which she plays a role as designated leader. She is a product of her society, choosing the monastic life as a higher call and embracing self-denial.[24] Yet Elizabeth has transcended her religious and secular worlds in some way. She is in touch with primal power, a power that recasts all conventions, norms, rules, and understandings of existence. What kind of woman is this? Who is she?

Only an embellished fragment of Elizabeth's life remains. Her full story is not known, her inner journey seemingly irrelevant to the community that has passed her narrative down through the centuries. What we have is a fantastical account of a woman, armed only with a cross, pummeling a dragon—more specifically, grabbing it by the head, spitting on it, and trampling it with her bare feet. This is a tough woman, one not constrained by polite ceremony. This is a fearless woman; she goes unafraid where others will not tread. *This is a woman who knows her own voice and uses it.* "Come out!" she commands the dragon. These are the very words Jesus used when casting out demons.

This woman also is well educated and well respected. She is powerful. She is influential enough to have received land from the emperor. Elizabeth is at once highly ambiguous and potent. We have only an icon and two words, "Come out!" Her voice comes down to us through the centuries in an imperative, in a command used by Jesus both to cast out demons and to raise Lazarus from the tomb. Elizabeth invites us to confront the destructive forces and the desire for full life in our own day.

Once we think about Elizabeth and other foremothers, we begin to see the fuller dimensions of their lives and faith. As we allow them to be who they are, these women can become gateways to wisdom for us. The process is reciprocal and relational. We cannot come to know them without coming to know ourselves. We cannot claim their wise faith as our heritage without beginning to discern its contours in our own lives. We discover the dynamics of our own faith in the process of reaching a place where we can hear our foremothers, even through the enforced silence of the tradition. In this place of listening to their voices we simultaneously allow them to "hear us into voice."[25] By discerning the faithful voices in women whom the Christian tradition largely has submerged and silenced, we learn something of our own voices and faith. There is no other route to receiving the gift of wisdom than that our foremothers in the Christian tradition offer: the practice of a complex, obstinate, and robust faith, a faith that does not fear the ambiguous spaces in ourselves and in our world where death and life are intimately intertwined. This faith is a resource we did not imagine for confronting our question as women of faith at the end of the twentieth century: Can the double quality of our Christian heritage as both death-dealing and life-giving become gift for us on our journey to God?

With our foremothers we may become able to say this: A religious tradition that has helped to create oppression can be subverted and transformed by its own more powerful resources; divine power is deeper and richer in a religious heritage than the institutional structures and officials that try to control it. Such are the insights of wise women.

Pause for Reflection

1. The Wisdom tradition of scripture appeals to our common human experience, to what brings fullness of life and peace for the entire community as the guide for making decisions. What appeals to you about using this criterion as a guide? What concerns you about it?

2. The Wisdom tradition of scripture calls on people of faith to practice discerning the action of God's Spirit in the midst of history and to cooperate with that action. Identify times when you sensed that what you were doing was congruent with God's Spirit active in your family, neighborhood, religious community, or work place.

3. When have you experienced patriarchy and androcentrism as obstacles in your life? In your mother's life? In your daughter's life? In your sister's life? In a friend's life?

4. Are there any women, alive or dead, whom you consider foremothers in faith? Who? What about them leads you to see them this way?

5. Review the story of Elizabeth the Wonder-Worker. Spend time with her icon. What do you see? Where and what are the ambiguities in Elizabeth's situation? Where do they lead you in your own life? Do any of the ambiguities in her story open up possibilities or stir your creative imagination about your own life situation? In what ways?

3

Listening to Our Longings

❧

Awakened Longing: Danger, Hope, and Paradox

"I'm standing by a river, dying of thirst." The woman's statement was honest, saturated with passion, and profoundly revealing. She was attuned to her deep but frustrated longing for God. She was aware that her longing was not being fed by her Christian heritage as she experienced it in her church. The woman did not know what to do with her intense longing and the pain of its frustration, or with her sense of dislocation from her Christian community. She was aware of her experience but unsure of what it meant, and so she was unclear about appropriate next steps on her journey of faith. But underneath her pain and frustration, hope was still alive in her. So on that cold winter evening she joined a gathering of women and uttered the truth of her experience in a powerful image.

I doubt the newcomer imagined her place of frustrated longing and dislocation that evening as a beginning point for wise faith. In the middle of the experience, especially as one first awakens to deep but frustrated longing, it feels anything but insightful or life-giving. Still, the very intensity of longing, the pain of frustration, and the sense of aloneness that dislocation from a community generates, as difficult as they are, in fact are spaces of possibility for encountering God. They are spaces of possibility because they lead to altered understandings of ourselves, our world, and our longing. They change us in irrevocable ways. But as with any contexts for transformation, our experiences of intense but frustrated longing contain both threat and promise. The threat of diminishment and loss and the promise of new and richer life are present equally in the open-ended nature of such experiences. We cannot predict or control how our senses of self, world, and longing will be altered— not once, but many times. Our experiences of frustrated longing make us keenly aware of our vulnerability as individuals, of our relationships, and of how much life is a process of discerning and cooperating with situations and forces that we do not know entirely and do not control.

As if the vulnerability that longing exposes in us were not enough, we also must contend with the paradoxical quality of longing or desire. Without desire we do not receive; yet, our desiring can be skewed, off the mark, or blocked in ways that interfere with receiving what we seek most dearly. This may be especially true in the life of faith. The story of Jesus' appearance to Mary Magdalene on Easter morning helps to illustrate.

Perfected Desire: Mary Magdalene (John 20:11–16)

> But Mary stood weeping outside the tomb. As she wept, she bent over to look into the tomb; and she saw two angels in white, sitting where the body of Jesus had been lying, one at the head and the other at the feet. They said to her, "Woman, why are you weeping?" She said to them, "They have taken away my Lord, and I do not know where they have laid him." When she had said this, she turned around and saw Jesus standing there, but she did not know that it was Jesus. Jesus said to her, "Woman, why are you weeping? Whom are you looking for?" Supposing him to be the gardener, she said to him, "Sir, if you have carried him away, tell me where you have laid him, and I will take him away." Jesus said to her, "Mary!" She turned and said to him in Hebrew, "*Rabbouni*" (which means Teacher).

The encounter between Jesus and Mary takes place on Easter morning. Mary had been to the tomb once already and finding it empty returned to tell the disciples. Now she has come back to the tomb with Peter and John. When the two of them look into the tomb where Jesus had been laid they see nothing, confirming what Mary Magdalene had told them earlier. Puzzled, John and Peter return to where the other disciples are. But Mary remains. She stands by the tomb weeping. She desires Jesus' presence and aches from his absence. Mary loves Jesus so much that she gladly would sit by his dead body until she died from her grief. To be dead with Jesus would be better than what she feels now. But Jesus' body is not in the tomb. She does not know where it is. Mary's situation typifies frustrated longing.

Intent on finding Jesus' body, Mary questions each figure whom she encounters. First she stoops and looks into the tomb. There she encounters two angels but does not recognize them as angels. Not even their question—"Woman, why are you weeping?"— jars her out of her grief-stricken longing into realization of the new reality she is confronting. Her response, "They have taken away my Lord, and I do not know where they have laid him," conveys quite clearly her longing for Jesus, but it is a desire focused on his corpse because, she believes, that is all that is left of him. She keeps looking for the body of the Jesus whom she knew. Mary Magdalene's desire is deep, her longing persistent. Her desire fuels her search.

After her interchange with the angels, Mary turns and encounters the Risen Jesus, but she does not know him. She mistakes him for the gardener, again misses the import of the questions about why she is weeping and for whom she is looking, and asks him where he has placed Jesus' body so that she can take it away. The scene and interchange at this point are full of irony. Here she is, confronted by Jesus, the focus of her longing, but she does not recognize him, precisely because she is looking for the corpse of the Jesus whom she knew. Such is the paradox of longing or desire: while it fuels our searching and focuses our attention, it also can limit what we see; and so, we can miss what we long for most deeply.

But then Jesus calls her by name, "Mary!" She *turns* again and recognizes him. This second turning is the fulcrum of the story. For in turning and recognizing Jesus when he calls her by name, Mary also turns or comes to herself. In the instant of call and response Mary's longing is transformed and fulfilled and she and her world are irrevocably changed.[1]

Mary Magdalene's story shows us how longing or desire works in a woman's life. She is unashamed of the range of human feeling that goes with her desire. She weeps openly, speaking to strangers through her tears. Her longing for Jesus is the criterion by which she chooses where to go and what to do. Precisely because she is so open about her desire, recognizes it, does not despise it, and acts on it, she is the first in John's gospel to encounter the Risen Lord. Yet her longing alone is not sufficient. Her desire is focused slightly off the mark—toward the body of the dead Jesus and not the Risen Lord—so at first she misses the object of her desire. Jesus is standing right there and she is looking for him with all her heart. But she only recognizes him *by his voice*, when he calls her by name.

Mary's longing is transformed and fulfilled in a surprising moment of encounter. This is true in our lives of virtually all our longings, not just our longing for God. Whenever we achieve what we have worked for or receive what we have sought, what comes to us does not come exactly as we expected it. And when it comes, we find that we are changed. Such moments are touching, sometimes funny, and sometimes embarrassing. But notice that Mary is not embarrassed over her failure to recognize Jesus. She does not lose the joy of encountering Jesus in injured pride, is not angry at him for not being what she expected. Instead, she hugs him, a fully embodied and relational response of utter delight. Mary Magdalene is not ashamed of her desire or the emotion and pain that go with it. Willing to accept longing as part of being human, and thereby accepting her status as a creature of God—a being that is not self-sufficient—Mary Magdalene is open to newness, including the utter newness of encountering a Risen Lord.

What comes through in Mary Magdalene's story is desire as a compass—longing that grounds integrity and provides focus and motivation, and yet expects the unexpected. Her story shows the real danger of frustrated longing—she might never have recognized the Risen Lord and might have died from her grief. But it also shows the possibility in frustrated longing—unimaginably gifted response to her deepest desire. If Mary Magdalene's story shows us anything, it shows us that desire does not lead one away from God; desire leads us to God. The experience of frustrated longing contains more possibilities for life than not desiring at all.

Inner and Outer Obstacles to Women's Longing

Mary Magdalene's story shows us longing or desire as an essential and potentially life-giving element in a woman's life. There is no religious journey, no journey of faith, without the desire for God. Learning to recognize, embrace, and name our desire is a courageous act. It takes courage to face a desiring that is so deep. It takes courage to face into the frustration of it. It takes courage and love to allow our desiring to be shifted ever so slightly as it is realized in response.

Growing in the courage and integrity necessary to experience human longing fully is quite sufficient as a developmental and spiritual task for any woman. Yet, as women in an androcentric and patriarchal world, we face inner and outer obstacles that can blindside us even before we can enter the experience of frustrated longing and discern its possibilities. For too many women these obstacles block them from ever coming to know this place of longing and frustration as one where wise faith may begin to grow.

Confronted with inner and outer obstacles to our longing, we respond in a range of ways when we become attuned to longing and its frustration. Some women begin to question themselves, their longings, and their struggle. "What is wrong with me?" a woman might write in her journal or ask a friend over coffee. "I know better than to get my hopes up," she may say to herself. Immediate self-questioning is an almost instinctive reaction for women raised in a society that is both sexist and psychologically oriented. Christian women formed in churches that hardly acknowledge the sin of sexism easily fall into the cultural trap of seeking the problem in themselves whenever they experience pain or encounter difficult situations.

Alternatively, some women, afraid or terrified by the experience of longing in themselves, flee from it into a diffuse, unfocused anger. They may project their discomfort outward. They may become hypercritical of the people and institutions around them. They may speak in strained, sometimes shrewish voices. Some people cringe in the presence of such women, alarmed by the force of their anger; or they flee, disturbed by what these women's anger evokes in them. Even worse, they may react angrily to women's pain, as the groaning files on domestic violence bear witness.

Still a third response to awakened awareness of longing and its frustration is a numbing, deadening depression. This too is a response of fear, especially in women for whom physical and psychological safety are paramount practical concerns in their lives.

Whether we respond to this wake-up call with self-doubt or anger or depression, our responses are reinforced by what we are told: that our longing and struggle evidence a flaw in us. "Just accept your proper place as a woman in the church." Or, "Sometimes you just have to sit in the pew and be quiet." Others suggest, "If you would just grow up you could leave the church and find something better." Or, "It is God's will." Or, "Face reality, the church is the way it is. Live with it."

Such responses to longing and struggle are not only unhelpful, they are damaging. They judge and dismiss women's experiences, denying their integrity and possibilities. Even worse, such responses block women's access to their own experiences and to their Christian tradition. Without these resources it becomes impossible for women who seek to be faithful to be nourished by their Christian heritage.

The experience of awakened but frustrated and often hurt-scarred longing is not the result of selfishness, psychological disturbance, or lack of realism. While our responses to awakened longing may be clumsy even to the point of destructiveness to self and others, we need to remember that our frustrated longing is an authentic spiritual experience with a long history in Christianity's biblical, historical, and theological traditions.[2] The ability to sustain hope-filled longing amid struggle in situations of oppression is one of the marks of a mature adult and one of the prerequisites for a dynamic spiritual life. Our experiences of hope-filled longing and struggle are faithful, not faithless. Our longing and struggle should be affirmed for their integrity, not condemned as aberrant. In multiple ways the experience of hope-filled longing and struggle can lead to deeper relationship with the reality toward which our Christian heritage points; it is a crucible where wise faith can be formed.

It is very difficult for women raised in the dominant Anglo cultures of the United States to allow themselves to become aware of deep but frustrated longing in themselves, let alone reach the point of understanding this experience as a context within which wisdom and faith can grow. Our socialization as women in a patriarchal culture that values control and accomplishment above all else leaves us with a decidedly ambivalent relationship to the experience of longing.

Women tend to be much better at desiring things for others than at desiring for themselves. Society gives women permission to want good things for parents, siblings, spouses, or children. It affirms women for sacrificing to help bring these desires to reality, especially the desires of the men in our lives. But the cost to women can be very high for wanting anything for ourselves. The cost for daring to seek what we desire is even higher.

Women learn the lessons very early. Unlike most little boys, a girl, if she chooses to do something she desires (and often if she dares even to voice a desire) and in any way provides less attention and care to others on account of it, hears very quickly and firmly the message of selfishness. The message is clear: selfishness will cost a woman love and care in her life. To desire something of our own will lead to abandonment and death. So quickly do girls learn, that by the time they reach first grade they play around the edges of the play field at recess, rarely daring to step out into the larger space that by common but unconscious understanding, from supervisor to youngest child, belongs to the boys. Such are the consequences of a patriarchal and androcentric society for women.[3]

Having learned early that they dare not desire something directly for themselves, some women stifle their longings or redirect them in socially acceptable ways. Other women live their longings through the lives of others. This has detrimental consequences both for the women and for those they love. When women project their desires onto others, they avoid having to acknowledge them or take responsibility for them. Neither do they have to acknowledge that they are confusing themselves and another person. So, for example, a mother may push her children in particular educational directions, convey forceful messages to them about how much she has sacrificed for them, or in other ways use her children to meet her own unacknowledged desires. Then, after living her longings by projecting them onto her children, she may feel bitterly betrayed when a child for whom she has "given so much" lets her down.[4]

A woman in the situation of projecting onto and living her longings through others has not developed the capacity to recognize and maintain appropriate boundaries between the self and others. This is understandable, given the socialization process that women undergo. But the cost to the woman and to those she loves is very high. The woman is not living her life. And ironically, the woman has kept her children from coming to know their own unique desires. Sadly, most women in this situation

remain unaware of what they have done and so cannot comprehend why their children resent them or flee. The same pattern of
denying one's own desires and projecting them onto others can
occur with spouses, friends, coworkers, or fellow members of religious communities.

Unable to acknowledge our own longings and desires, many of
us are caught in cycles of self-loathing, self-pity, and rage that are
directed alternately inward toward ourselves and outward toward
children, spouses, parents, or colleagues. Unless we discriminate
between our longings for ourselves and the genuine longings that
we have for those whom we love, we may confuse the two. We can
forget that we genuinely desired something for a spouse or child
or parent or sibling. We may deny that we made the choice to give
up advanced education for a spouse, or postponed a career for a
child, or accepted a ministry other than the one we would have
chosen for the good of our religious community. Women in this
predicament become caught between denial of desire and raging
desire. They may destroy themselves and others with the acids
of resentment and recrimination. If we as women do not begin to
face these patterns and exchange them for better ways of being
ourselves and being with others, our lives can become encrusted
in layers of enmeshed relationships, buried beneath the accumulated callouses of disappointment, distorted through fantasies of
a life without any limits.

Little in women's economic and social realities encourages us
to find a new way of being. Few women have economic resources
of their own, despite working longer hours than men both inside
and outside the home.[5] Social pressures, including for some
women the threat of physical violence, are major deterrents to
change. It is difficult to live in a different way, to become a different kind of person, when most messages one receives reinforce a
patriarchal and woman-denying world so well.

Women's Longing for God

What is true of particular desires—for a career, a chance for creative fulfillment, a particular kind of home—is also true of the longing for God. Given our situations, many women are ambivalent about

whether God cares about us or not. We may be uncomfortable about the desire that arises in us for God when God has been presented to us as sanctioning our subservience and submission to men and male-dominated institutions and as the source of all that happens to us, including our pain. Why would one long for a God who is the source of so much pain? As one woman put in when she came to a women's reflection group: "My week was so bad that I thought about killing myself. But then I thought, 'I'd be a failure in heaven too.'"

Even when a woman begins to recognize her longing for God, it can terrify her. She may not want to face her desire for God when it is overwhelmingly unfulfilled. This woman's deep longing is powerful and fearsome precisely because she has known so little fulfillment of longing in her life, knows so well the danger and/or futility of desiring anything for herself, and wearies of the ambivalence that acknowledging her own desires creates for her. Deep longing is painful too when a woman interprets it, generally inaccurately, as a sign that she should continue on a self-denying, self-deprecating path in life. For example, a woman may interpret the sacrament of marriage to mean that she should remain with and submit to an abusive spouse. Facing her desire for God is difficult and painful for a woman precisely because it calls her to see and experience and live her life differently. A woman's desire for the living God undercuts her world.

Neither the religious nor the secular world takes women's desires seriously. Desire, especially desire that arises out of the shared pain of those who are not allowed voice or status in a society, is too powerful, too subversive, too dangerous for patriarchal institutions to recognize. Patriarchal religious traditions instead hold up stories of women's desire that have negative consequences: Eve's eating the apple in Genesis, Herod's wife desiring the head of John the Baptist, the uncontrollable desire that brought the woman caught in adultery to her sorry state before Jesus. Overwhelmingly, the tradition has presented women's desires as bad unless directed, guided, and controlled by men.[6] Given the negative messages that women receive about themselves and their desires and the ambivalence that a powerful experience of longing can evoke in a person, it is easy to understand why many accept the interpretation of women's desire as problematic, if not actively evil. But the consequence to us of holding our desire this way is disastrous.

Alternative Ways of Holding Our Longing

Patriarchal forces in church and society have never succeeded entirely in convincing women that their desires were evil or in destroying the deep intuition that women's desire may be a genuine path to God. Desire is subtly and not so subtly present in both scriptural and secular texts. The stories of two women—the woman bent over from Luke's gospel, and a nineteenth-century Irish immigrant to the United States, Margaret Gaffney Haughery—offer alternative ways of relating to the experience of desire in our lives.

Desire Embraced:
The Woman Bent Over (Luke 13:10–17)

> Now he was teaching in one of the synagogues on the sabbath. And just then there appeared a woman with a spirit that had crippled her for eighteen years. She was bent over and was quite unable to stand up straight. When Jesus saw her, he called her over and said, "Woman, you are set free from your ailment." When he laid his hands on her, immediately she stood up straight and began praising and thanking God. But the leader of the synagogue, indignant because Jesus had cured on the sabbath, kept saying to the crowd, "There are six days on which work ought to be done; come on those days and be cured, and not on the sabbath day." But the Lord answered him and said, "You hypocrites! Does not each of you on the sabbath untie his ox and his donkey from the manger, and lead it away to give it water? And ought not this woman, a daughter of Abraham whom Satan bound for eighteen long years, be set free from this bondage on the sabbath day?" When he said this, all his opponents were put to shame; and the entire crowd was rejoicing at all the wonderful things that he was doing.

It is very easy to miss the woman bent over.[7] The writer of Luke uses her story to intensify the conflict between the synagogue leaders and Jesus. The synagogue leader missed her. He saw in her healing only a seeming affront to the Law. We do not know her name. We do not know why she was "bent over and was quite unable to stand up straight." We do not know why she came to the synagogue. We know only that this woman was able to respond unhesitatingly to God's healing power after eighteen years of pain and deformity.

At first glance we might attribute her lack of hesitation to God's power alone. That move puts us into the synagogue leader's shoes, however, missing the woman and seeing only a battle of divine powers. That move also does violence to her freedom and insults God's love for her.

The woman's story is told mainly between the lines of a text that tells us three things: 1) the woman who was bent over for eighteen years was at the synagogue where Jesus was teaching; 2) when Jesus spoke to her and touched her she "immediately stood up straight"; and, 3) she "began praising and thanking God." Between the lines of this minimal data we see a woman who had desired God and healing for a long time. We also see a woman who was attuned to her desire in a way that left her spirit free and made her capable of responding to newness in her life.

As anyone who has suffered with it knows, chronic pain or disability must be embraced after a while; it can become so familiar that it seeps unknown into one's spirit and subtly and not so subtly possesses one's standpoint and shapes one's perspective. When chronic pain abates, the sufferer can become disoriented, not knowing who she is without it. Yet we are confronted in Luke's story with a woman who unhesitatingly stood up straight when offered healing after eighteen years, a woman whose disability, while it drained her strength, did not shackle her freedom or cripple her desire. How was this possible?

The woman bent over was able to experience what happened to her and all the feelings that went with it without letting them clog and clot her spirit. She did not identify herself with her deformity or her pain. She was able to experience pain, to let it move through her without letting it define her. She was able to accept her situation without being determined by it. She had inner freedom in relation to her situation. This was not a false sense of inner freedom that said she was not touched by her deformity; she was disabled, drained of strength, and she knew it. The freedom that she possessed was genuine—honest and accurate in assessing self and situations. Such freedom is characterized by a gentle and compassionate self-acceptance.

This freedom, this way of holding herself gently, made it possible for the woman bent over to hear and to respond when Jesus called her. When he said, "Woman, you are set free from your ailment," she immediately stood up straight. She did not hesitate. This wise woman was open to receiving God's gift of healing because she was open to her life, all of it, the parts she liked and the parts she did not like. She was open because she dared to desire God and to desire healing. The woman bent over knew how to move freely with grace. She knew how to live with her longing for God. She knew how to let it fund her life instead of sap life from her, as did the deformity that drained her strength during the years of waiting.

How did she cultivate this ability, this woman whose deformity for eighteen years prevented her body from moving freely? The woman befriended her longing for God. Acknowledging her longing, becoming aware of all its dimensions, noticing them without judging them, accepting the full range of human emotions that goes with longing: all of these are implied in the woman's capacity to respond to Jesus "immediately."

Befriending her longing made it real and present but prevented it from becoming a tyrannous or loathsome force in her life. Befriending her longing helped the woman gain perspective and proportion about herself, her situation, and her world. Befriending her longing kept her from slipping into self-loathing, resentment, cynicism, or blind rage.

Befriending does not mean soul-deadening acquiescence or submission to infirmity, abuse, injustice, or anything else that diminishes life. It does mean relating to oneself and one's situation, to one's thoughts and feelings, longings, and desires in a way that increases perspective and perceptiveness, that awakens possibilities and a range of freedom that one has not known until now.

Think about the woman bent over. Despite social and religious prejudice she seems to have had that gentle acceptance of herself, true freedom. Despite all the physical and social evidence to the contrary, this woman was deeply in touch within herself with her longing for God. She recognized the irony of her situation, praising God in the prayers of a tradition that taught that those with infirmities were being punished for their sins. But this woman was in touch with her heritage at a deeper level than popular bias. She was connected to it through her own deep-seated longing for God, a longing that came to expression in her need to praise God. Trusting that need, trusting her longing for God, she acted on it, and the ritual of praising—however foolish it may have looked to her neighbors, and at times to herself—kept the woman who was bent over cleansed and open and ready to receive God's healing when it came to her through Jesus. The woman bent over knew how to experience her experience, to befriend her longing for God and for healing, to grow wise through her experience.

Frustrated Desire Transformed: Margaret Gaffney Haughery (1813–82)[8]

The woman bent over illustrates intense longing that does not become demand or obsession in one's life. Hers is a story of longing as an essential element of freedom, of full personhood. Her story also is optimistic for us, because in the end her longing is satisfied—"she stood up straight" and "began praising and thanking God." Biblical stories, especially biblical stories of healing, may appear easy because they present decisive, divine action so clearly. The situation of later historical figures may better approximate our own. Take, for example, a nineteenth-century Irish immigrant to the United States, Margaret Gaffney Haughery. Margaret's story confronts us with frustrated longing. It confronts us with the need to discern the difference between the transformation of frustrated longing and the crippling of the human person, in her life and in our own.

Like many other nineteenth-century American Catholic women, Margaret Gaffney Haughery was an immigrant from Ireland. Her family migrated to the United States in 1818 when Margaret was five, and settled in Baltimore. In 1822 both her parents died in the yellow fever epidemic. Orphaned at age nine she ended up in domestic service, the most common occupation of Irish-American Catholic women. Margaret never learned to read or write.

In 1835, at the age of twenty-two, she married Charles Haughery, a young Irishman. They moved to New Orleans shortly after the wedding. In 1836, soon after the birth of a sickly daughter, Margaret's husband and daughter both died. Widowed and bereaved at the age of twenty-three, Margaret was left alone once again to find her way in the world.

For a while she worked as a laundress. Then she began to assist the Sisters of Charity in the Poydras Orphan Asylum, making her home at the orphanage. She liked being with these children who, like herself, had no families. From the savings gleaned from her laundry work, Margaret bought a few cows and started a dairy, which prospered. She peddled milk through the streets in the early mornings, giving away more than she sold. From the proceeds of her dairy she helped build more orphanages. Margaret nursed people during yellow fever epidemics and piloted rafts during Mississippi flood time to rescue people.

In 1858 Margaret received the D'Aquin Bakery in payment of a debt. She gave up the dairy and enlarged the bakery, employing forty men to whom she served lunch daily. She is credited with the establishment of the first steam bakery in the South and with the innovation of packaged crackers. Her bakery became the city's largest export business at a time when New Orleans was one of the great ports of the world. Her success, however, did not change her habits. She daily sat outside her office and dispensed sympathy, counsel, bread, and monetary gifts according to the needs of those who came to her.

During the Civil War, Margaret conducted sewing and knitting groups, assisted with free markets three days a week, and cared for soldiers' families. She nursed sick soldiers of both North and South. After the war her business expanded, despite the disturbances of Reconstruction.

Apparently Margaret kept no records of her largess. As she earned money she dispensed it wherever she found need. In the 1870s and 1880s, her attention turned particularly to care for the elderly. In the three years between 1873 and 1876 she gave $9,000 for repairs to the Home for the Aged conducted by the Little Sisters of the Poor alone.

Fearful of publicity and embarrassed by thanks, Margaret habitually cautioned friends not to tell of her gifts. Only at her death did the City of New Orleans learn the extent of her munificence. She made her last gifts through her will, stipulating large sums for ten institutions, including those of Protestant and Jewish affiliation. February 9 is Margaret Haughery Day in New Orleans. She also is known as the Bread Woman of New Orleans.

Margaret Gaffney Haughery desired simple things in her life: a spouse, a family, people to love and by whom to be loved. With the death of her parents, spouse, and child, Margaret's life was, on one level, a life of grief and unfulfilled desire. There is no way to erase the pain and effects of being orphaned at the age of nine, widowed at twenty-two, and having buried her only child before she was twenty-three. We cannot pretend that Margaret's psyche and spirit were not marked by these events. The question we must ask is how to interpret what Margaret did when, after the death of her husband and her child, she was alone again in the world.

One interpretation of Margaret is that she lost herself, that she became a woman whose entire life of self-giving service was a desperate effort to cover up the pain of her losses. There is another interpretation, however. Perhaps Margaret's frustrated longing for family was transformed in ways she would not and could not have planned.

Margaret left no journal, no letters that reveal her psyche and soul, so we must interpret her life from the evidence we have. Having lost her own child, Margaret chose to live with orphans. Having entered the work force at age nine, her education disrupted, she built orphanages so that children would have a place to live and be able to go to school. Orphaned child of poverty, Margaret became a very successful entrepreneur. As if she had nothing to lose, Margaret took risks in her life: she entered an entirely new business at the age of forty-five, piloted rescue rafts on the Mississippi during floods, and nursed the sick during yellow fever epidemics. Her final bequests continued a practice of generosity that went back to distributing free milk and feeding her bakery workers.

How shall we interpret Margaret's life around the issue of longing? Given all that she did, I think that at some level a deep longing for her parents, her dead husband, and her infant daughter were constant companions in her life. What had happened to her could not be undone. Yet she did not seek to reverse or escape the events of her life by remarrying, moving West, or turning to prostitution, all of which were options, given her situation. Instead, the evidence suggests that her unfulfilled longings were transformed in ways that allowed them to become bridges of compassionate relationship to other human beings. Margaret chose to live with orphans, to provide for them what their dead parents could not—personal presence as well as education. Margaret did not horde her money but shared her abundance. She gave away what came to her, implying an inner knowledge that her abundance was gift and not possession. Finally, she was not afraid to act, to put herself into new and dangerous situations.

In the end, I think it truer to see Margaret's relationship to her own desires and their frustrations as a resource for her. Knowing loss, she did not despise her own or others' inner weaknesses. Having endured great pain, she was not afraid of her own longing. This made it possible for her to be open to other people, to be generous personally and financially, to love despite the pain of loving that she knew from her own experience.

Margaret's story makes clear in graphic terms that encountering frustrated longings is part of life. Her story illustrates how one woman negotiated frustrated longing in her life and did so in a way that kept her from dying of grief. Margaret's story suggests how our deep desires and longings—even when they are frustrated—can be transformed, how possibility can emerge even in situations of irretrievable loss.

Accepting that longing is part of our life and that some longings will be frustrated, we can encounter our experiences of frustrated longing in relationship to our Christian heritage in new ways. At the very least, we become able to acknowledge and explore these experiences rather than denying or prejudging them.

The Practice of Listening to Our Longing

To listen to our longing is not easy. Doing so involves disciplines that are physical, psychological, and spiritual. Above all else, listening to our longing evokes an act of faith from us as women: that we are of value, that we are worth the time and energy to notice our experience, to sit with it and to explore its meaning, trusting that God is with us in it.

To listen to our longing requires that we not hide from it, whether we hide through compulsive or impulsive behaviors such as eating, spending, talking, cleaning, socializing, working, and such, or through willed conformity to what we think our religious tradition expects. It requires that we pay attention to our experiences by taking the time to notice them with all their inner and outer dimensions, their ambiguities and ambivalences. This involves taking the time to breathe deeply and to pay attention to all the sensations in our bodies, the feelings in our hearts, the thoughts running through our minds. It involves corralling all our judgments and biases about ourselves, our church, and our world, while we explore freshly our particular, concrete experiences of longing, dislocation, frustration, and hope. Listening to our longing requires us as women to trust that psychic and emotional discomfort will not destroy us, to trust that we are not the problem, to avoid the temptation to dichotomous us/them, black/white, good/bad ways of reducing and distorting reality.

To practice listening to our longing requires being receptive to ourselves. It leads to a growing awareness of who we are, of all the dimensions of ourselves and our experiences, and at the same time, a growing capacity to refrain from judging. Gentle presence to ourselves is crucial. For how can we know if God is with us if we are not willing to be with ourselves? To practice listening to our longings requires learning how to narrate our experiences and to listen to ourselves as we do it. Even better, tell and listen with friends.

Listening to our longing involves gentle, attending presence to ourselves, a cherishing of our lives, a trust deeper than whatever harm or hurt we have endured. Listening to our longing moves us to name our desires and to narrate our acts of resistance. Listening to our longing, we begin to find our voices.

☙◈❧

Pause for Reflection

1. Draw a time line of your life, with a section for each decade. Divide the last ten-year section of your life into two five-year periods. On the time line identify a deep desire that you had at each point in your life. What happened to that desire? Was it fulfilled? Was it squelched? What has been your relationship to desire in your life?

2. "Standing by a river, dying of thirst" symbolizes the experience of women who are not being nurtured by their Christian heritage. Think about your own life to this point. Describe a time when you have felt unnourished by your Christian heritage or your particular church, perhaps a situation you identified in reflection question 1 from the first chapter. Describe the experience as fully as you can.

Allow yourself to be present to that experience again; place yourself there. Be aware of your thoughts and feelings in that situation.

Does the image of "standing by a river, dying of thirst" capture the experience for you? If not, does another image capture it better? Let an image hold your experience for you.

Write about "standing by a river, dying of thirst" (or about your own image). How does the image speak to you about the longings and desires and frustrations and fears and hopes that it contains? What does it tell you about your longings for God? your desires for yourself and those you love? your frustrations with your religious tradition or Christian community?

Take the powerful parts of this reflection with you into prayer.

3. Mary Magdalene knew her desire for Jesus as the compass of her life. It allowed her to sort and sift the important from the unimportant, the truly dangerous from the merely frightening, the counterfeit from the authentic. Think about your own life journey. What have been some of the compasses of your life? What has your life been like when you did not have a compass?

4. The woman bent over befriended her longing. Have you ever befriended another person? What are the dynamics of befriending? What would happen to you now if you befriended your own longing?

5. Reread the story of Margaret Gaffney Haughery. What attracts you in this story? How does this foremother's experiences of life and of faith resonate with your own? What does her story make you notice in your own? What does her story lead you to grieve in your own? What does her story lead you to hope for in your own?

4

Embracing Frustrated Longing: A Woman's Act of Faith

❧

Facing Frustrated Longing

The realization that her longing for God is not being nourished by her church, that she is "standing by a river, dying of thirst," comes to a woman in different ways at different times in her life. For some, it begins with the startling realization that a devotional practice that for so long provided comfort and sustenance no longer does. The rosary beads or novenas or meditative sitting or reading of scripture no longer connect her to the divine. A support group that carried her through difficult times now feels burdensome, its members strangers. The startling realization leaves her unbalanced, dry, doubting, even angry.

For others, the awareness of growing thirst begins with a nagging dissatisfaction. Perhaps an awareness dawns that her work as a volunteer catechist or Sunday School teacher is not valued. Perhaps it is the repeated experience of having her ideas ignored when offered in a parish council meeting, but then hearing them received as wonderful suggestions when repeated by a male member of the council. Perhaps the dissatisfaction comes in realizing how little she knows of scripture or theology or church history, especially how little she knows of the experience and thought of women in the Christian tradition. Perhaps the realization flashes into consciousness when she finds herself in conflict with the parish priest and knows deep inside that she cannot receive justice. Perhaps it comes from sitting through liturgies week after week that drain life and cut her off from the very experience of God's love she went there seeking.

For some women a powerful contrast experience leads them to religiously inspired judgment that becomes the source of the realization that their relationship to the Christian tradition is not feeding them. Injustice against and abuse of women in church and society provide the contrast for many. The stories are legion: the story of the priest who tells the wife of the alcoholic that she should go to the tavern with her husband; the story of the priest who tells the woman with the ruptured uterus that she cannot have a hysterectomy because it is against the church's moral teaching; the story of the bishop who tells his clergy after a day's conference with an expert on pedophilia that prayer can solve the problem; the story of the mother comforting her daughter after the new priest in the parish bans girls from being altar servers; the story of the small group of families that leaves the parish after a new pastor dismantles the liturgy committee and fires the pastoral staff; the story of the diocese that closes its inner-city schools because Catholic students are not attending them and they do not provide income or members; the story of the sister who is silenced and sent to study "traditional theology" in Europe because she dares to say that the way the environment is treated and the way that women are treated are connected.[1] These and the thousands of other stories that women tell each other when we are alone and can speak candidly illustrate the contrast between what women often experience and what Christianity's preaching of God's love for all promises.

For some women it is not dissatisfaction or the voicing of a prophetic "no" in response to a situation that leads to the realization that their relationship to their religious heritage is dislocated. For these women, the realization comes through the awakening of a deep desire. One experiences a call to ordained ministry that is confirmed by people she knows and denied by designated institutional leaders. Another is transformed by an intense and intimate encounter with God that recasts every other relationship and project. Another thrills in a professional accomplishment and finds herself drawn to desire more in all dimensions of her life, aware that rebuilding relationships will be a slow process. Another gives birth to a female child and in the core of her being commits to finding a community that will support and empower her daughter's religious life, though she has never known such a community. Another creates art of great beauty and desires companions who will appreciate it. Still another savors joy in her life and longs for the language and the context in which she can voice it.

Whether arising from startling dislocation, dissatisfaction, contrast experience, or desire, the realization that her relationship to the Christian tradition is not right, that she is "standing by a river, dying of thirst," comes to a woman unbidden. It forces her to notice the depth of her longing for God and the pain of having that longing frustrated. How she responds to that experience of longing and frustration is crucial to the development of her spiritual life.

The intense experiences of longing and frustrated longing generate a range of reactions in us, among them sorrow, resignation, rage, fear, anger, confusion, acceptance, and disillusionment. Denying any or all of these feelings is destructive to a woman's spiritual journey and to her integrity as a human being. The first step toward wise faith is the willingness to notice and acknowledge the intense experiences of longing and frustrated longing, with the full range of feelings and thoughts that are part of them.

Women can become frightened at this stage of their spiritual development because conflict and dissonance are so uncomfortable for many. The temptation is to run away from the experience through busyness, extensive involvement with people, or rigid adherence to a technique of prayer or devotion that worked in the past. None of these strategies will work in the end.

The journey to wise faith invites each one to feel her feelings, not as the sum total of her life but as an essential and gifted dimension of it. Feelings, deep human emotions, are our embodied, holistic response to life situations. They are potentially sources of insight and empathy for ourselves and for others. But they can be this for us only if we are willing to experience them.

If she is willing to attend to her experience of dislocation and to acknowledge and move through the range of human emotions that are so crucial to the experience of intense but frustrated longing, a woman likely will enter a time of reexamination and reflection. The fruits of that reflection may generate a new round of strong emotions and a sense of general "dis-ease" as well. A woman may find the ways that she has understood and interpreted her life until now to be insufficient. She may look more closely at how she has lived and the choices she has made. Such reflection can generate grief as well as satisfaction, sorrow and resentment as well as joy and peace. A woman may sense a desire to focus her gifts and talents more deliberately. Taking steps in this direction can empower a woman at the same time that it creates strain by changing her role in her family, religious community, friendships, church, or work place. This time of reexamination often leads a woman to turn a more critical eye to all authority structures, especially those of her religious tradition.

Whatever shape this time of reexamination and reflection takes, it disrupts a woman's life, generates discontent with whatever script she is now living, and poses the threat of loss and pain. It creates a crisis time in her life, a time of redefinition, of reimagining, of reinterpreting her life, of choosing to act differently. Whether occasioned by events that she calls positive or events she calls negative matters little. What has happened to the woman cannot be undone. The boundaries of her world have been cracked, the possibilities for destructive choices or richer life confront her. Which she will choose depends very much on the woman's willingness to experience her longing deeply and to endure, even embrace her frustration. In these two acts, wise faith begins to grow.

Longing and Frustrated Longing as Hope and Resistance

Experiencing longing, and enduring or even embracing its frustration are acts of integrity if they contain promise of some kind, possibilities that undercut the present even as they spur the imagination toward a better future. Often for us as women that promise is our sense of the presence of something powerful in the Christian heritage, even when we cannot identify it or voice it in words. We sense a powerful something that can soothe, heal, challenge, support, and empower us. This intuitive sense connects us to the wisdom we believe the Christian heritage contains, to the insight and affirmation it can offer us. This intuitive sense that there is something for women in the Christian tradition funds our longing and endurance. It keeps us "standing by the river," often in the face of massive evidence suggesting that walking away from the Christian tradition is the only act of integrity left to us. This intuitive sense that the Christian heritage can nourish us leads us to trust our longing and not to label it childish or self-deceptive. This intuitive sense allows us to see the hope in our longing.

Our very act of hope-filled longing—never mind our expression of our desire—is an act of resistance and disbelief. Put simply, our longing in and of itself is an act of resistance to the ideas and practices that have, in the name of Christianity, demeaned and destroyed women's being: our bodies, our spirits, our dignity. Our longing leads us to reject everything from the tradition and everyone in the tradition that has told us in so many ways that women are less, inferior, defective, not made in the image of God. Our longing is not blind to androcentrism—the ways reality has been defined normatively as the experiences and achievements of men. Our longing is not blind to the patriarchy—the teaching that deferring to the authority of the fathers is best for all—that permeates the Christian tradition and our particular denominations and local congregations. The longing is not blind to and does not forgive the injustice that women suffer in the name of Christianity. Our longing is an affirmation that the Christian heritage is more than what it has said about and done to women up to now, more than the attitudes, words, behaviors, norms, and rules embodied in current structures and expressed by some formally designated leaders.

This act of longing and hope, this expression of our desire, is also an act of trust in ourselves and in the women who have preceded us in the Christian community. We trust that neither they nor we can be dismissed as being without wisdom. They were more than victims of a patriarchal society and church, even though they often were that too. They should not all be dismissed as being guilty of massively alienated consciousness. Our hope-filled longing and resistance constitute an act of trust in the women who have come before us in the tradition, trust that their lives of faith were meaningful and that they mattered. Brave, talented, loving, ambitious women came before us in the tradition and received powerful resources from its wisdom and store of images. Our active longing and hope take these foremothers of faith seriously and seek access to their resources.

Frustrated and Hope-Filled Longing as Faith

A frustrated but hope-filled longing for God expressed through resistance and desire: this act of faith characterizes many Christian women today. Such an act of faith takes courage, a courage often accompanied by feelings of foolishness and doubt. We have all sensed, if not spoken, the hard questions that come when we face our frustration and sense of foolishness, experiencing ourselves dislocated and on the edge of our Christian tradition. Is it possible for this tradition to offer us something in light of the androcentrism and patriarchy that mark the history of Christianity? Can it nourish us in light of the current abuse of women, justified on Christian grounds and in the name of God? Why bother to maintain any connection to the Christian heritage or to the institutional church in light of the overwhelming abuse and devaluing that women have known there?

Honesty requires us to face these questions. When we have faced our deep longing for God and endured the frustration of having it blocked and not fed by our Christian tradition, we cannot avoid them. However we phrase the questions, we are, at bottom, asking this: Can Christianity be a viable Wisdom tradition for women? Can it mediate healing and liberation? Can it motivate resistance to oppression? Can it empower women's self-worth and human dignity? Can it fund constructive critique and spur creative imagination in our lives? And, if it can do these things, how can it do so for me?

We ask these questions in our own context at the end of the twentieth century, informed as we are by concepts of the dignity of the individual, human rights, and feminist consciousness. The questions are particular to our time and circumstances, but faith as resistance and desire runs deep in the Jewish and Christian traditions. Seeing it in the stories of our foremothers can help us to know it better in our own lives.

Resistance and Desire as Faith:
Woman with a Hemorrhage
(Mark 5:25–34 and Luke 8:40–48)

[As he went to the house of Jairus] a large crowd followed him and pressed in on him. Now there was a woman who had been suffering from hemorrhages for twelve years. She had endured much under many physicians, and had spent all that she had; and she was no better, but rather grew worse. She had heard about Jesus and came up behind him in the crowd and touched his cloak, for she said, "If I but touch his clothes, I will be made well." Immediately her hemorrhage stopped; and she felt in her body that she was healed of her disease. Immediately aware that power had gone forth from him, Jesus turned about in the crowd and said, "Who touched my clothes?" And his disciples said to him, "You see the crowd pressing in on you; how can you say, 'Who touched me?'" He looked all around to see who had done it. But the woman, knowing what had happened to her [and seeing that she could not remain hidden], came in fear and trembling, fell down before him, and told him the whole truth [declared in the presence of all the people why she had touched him, and how she had been immediately healed]. He said to her, "Daughter, your faith has made you well; go in peace, and be healed of your disease."

The woman with the hemorrhage is an outcast because of her physical disability. Her womb bleeds. That very part of her being that establishes a woman's value in her culture betrays her, pollutes her, marks her as outside the community. It is no wonder that she seeks to remain anonymous, to others and to herself.

And yet, even after twelve years of unsuccessful treatment, which has brought her only impoverishment and continued ostracization, something in her still hopes. This outcast's desire for health and wholeness is stronger than despair. So under the protection of a milling crowd, her anonymity guarded by numbers, she touches Jesus' garment—and she is healed.

What power this bleeding woman embodies! Despite her steadily deteriorating condition over twelve years she continues to resist and to desire. What does she resist? For one thing, she resists seemingly inevitable fate. She will not accept what twelve years time and innumerable specialists have told her, that nothing can be done. For another, she resists society's judgment of her. In her day and her society, a menstruating woman was considered unclean and polluting. A woman was to withdraw and separate herself from society during her menses. To hemorrhage without ceasing for twelve years suggested severe punishment from God for sin, a punishment that was doubly harmful because it demanded isolation on the woman's part and polluted anyone with whom she came into contact. Yet the woman resists this explanation of her condition. She also resists the temptation to despair. The woman with the hemorrhage does not give up. She continues to desire healing. She desires it so strongly that she risks retribution from the crowd when she joins them to find Jesus. She desires healing so strongly that she risks losing her life.

Resistance and desire, a combined orientation offered to us by this wise woman! It keeps her going against all odds. It protects her dreams and motivates her will when nobody and nothing confirm her choices and actions. This orientation, born and honed in her experience of suffering and her capacity to imagine better, propels her to Jesus. She touches his garment, and he is conscious at once that "healing power has gone forth from him."

Think about this language. Power goes out from him. The woman with the hemorrhage claims healing. She, the polluted one, touches Jesus, the one whom the whole crowd recognizes as being anointed with God's power. She takes healing power from the one who, in the conventions of her day, should have been most reviled by the touch of a hemorrhaging woman. But she resists conventions that strip her of her humanity; she draws healing from Jesus. She experiences God's healing power by touching Jesus.

After she is healed and tells her story, Jesus points out to her that her faith has cured her. He does not say, "Because of your faith I have cured you," or "Because of your faith God has healed you"; he says, "Your faith has made you well." Faith in this woman is that dual combination of resistance and desire, and Jesus wants the woman to notice the power of such faith. He wants her to notice that the power of her desire for healing—thriving despite all the times the world dismissed and contradicted it—has cured her.

Resistance and Desire as the Thirst for Justice:
Lucy Burns (1879–1966)

Resistance and desire are not the province of biblical foremothers alone. The story of Lucy Burns exemplifies the same combination.[2] She was one of the few religiously affiliated women in the radical wing of the suffrage movement in the United States. Lucy holds the distinction of having spent more time in jail than any other American suffragist. She also was and remained a devout Roman Catholic all her life.

Born and raised in an upper-class Irish family in Brooklyn, Lucy abandoned her graduate education to join the Suffrage Movement in England. She brought back to the United States the "militant" techniques that she learned there from Sylvia Pankhurst—giving public speeches, disrupting meetings, resisting arrest, and going on hunger strikes when imprisoned. Despite conflict within the ranks of the Suffrage Movement itself, despite the opposition of the American Catholic hierarchy, despite the opposition or disinterest of most other Roman Catholic women at the time, Lucy persevered in her efforts. Beaten, imprisoned, force-fed, she did not give up. When national suffrage finally passed in 1919, Lucy Burns and coworker Alice Paul were most credited with bringing it about.

Lucy Burns wed her commitment to women's suffrage and her use of radical suffragist tactics to her deep Catholic faith at a time when most Catholic bishops, led by Cardinal Gibbons, attacked the movement and made no secret of their hostility toward it, and when most Catholic women of her class opposed the vote for women. She placed seeking suffrage for women over a career as an academic. She knew her desire, her thirst for justice, and it allowed her to endure abuse, misunderstanding, physical pain, and oppression for nearly a decade, during which she worked to gain the power of the vote for women.

The clash between Lucy's thirst for justice and the hierarchy's position on women's suffrage must have generated disillusionment in her. Yet Lucy did not leave the church or lessen her practice of prayer. She negotiated her disillusionment and remained deeply faithful.

Lucy, like the woman bent over, like Mary Magdalene, like the woman with the hemorrhage, like Margaret Gaffney Haughery, and like Elizabeth the Wonder-Worker, knew what most of us know but may not put into words: the Christian faith is deeper and bigger than any particular articulation of it by any particular leadership or interest group at any particular time. Knowing this, Lucy was able to be simultaneously critical of her own religious tradition and to draw upon its powerful resources to sustain her.

Lucy used a particular interpretive strategy in approaching her religious tradition: a strategy of suspicion. She questioned the tradition, noticing the ways it did not fit her experience, the ways it was used to deny her dignity, the ways it was used to rationalize injustice. But she did not stop there. Lucy went on to use a strategy of retrieval: approaching her religious tradition in a way that allowed her to find in it life-giving and creative resources for making her own and others' lives better.

Lucy Burns was able to relate to her Catholic tradition with both suspicion and the expectation of finding resources for her life. This allowed her to follow the call of justice in working for women's suffrage and to be nourished and supported for that work by her Catholic faith and heritage even when the institutional church did not support her.

Lucy's thirst for justice, rooted in her Catholic faith, led her to a critically creative and adaptive strategy for being a Catholic woman in her day and time. But it is a strategy for faithful adults, not for people who are children in terms of faith. To be able to criticize our tradition when our best judgment is that it is being misused and misinterpreted; to be able to endure opposition from people we care about and from formal institutional leadership; to trust our thirst for justice when others do not see the situation as we see it, and still to be able to dive deep into the life-giving wells of our tradition—this is what wise women can do.

Resistance and desire are essential elements of faith for women. They require that we ask our hard questions about God and our Christian heritage and our particular denominations and not settle for easy answers. They require that we take our own experience and the experience of other women seriously. They ask that we hold our tradition as valuable, despite the devastating legitimacy of the critiques of patriarchy that feminist theologians and historians have leveled against Christianity and its treatment of women.[3] Resistance and desire invite us to trust our sense that

that same tradition has mediated life for women and can still do so. This faith asks that we continue to experience our deep longing for God and endure its frustration because we sense that the tradition has more to offer than slow death. Our parched souls have been soothed, sometimes if only through promise and our own desire. However little we and our foremothers have received, we sense the more that is in the Christian heritage and we seek it. This is the faith of resistance and desire, a faith at once ruthlessly honest and deeply hopeful. This is a faith that calls women to wisdom.

That call to wisdom comes in our knowing that in our longing and frustration, which also are hope and resistance and trust, the boundaries of our world have been cracked open by our realizations of dislocation, discontent, prophetic judgments, or deep desires. This crack creates a space for newness, a room for God's grace to work, a space within which our relationship to the Christian heritage will be transformed.

An Invitation to Renegotiate Relationship

Our experience of hope-filled, frustrated longing becomes the starting point on the journey to wise faith for many women. It becomes the starting point when we come to know it as an invitation to a total renegotiation of our relationship to our Christian heritage. The Christian tradition has honored such renegotiations— reimagining, hearing, feeling, and acting in new ways—throughout its history. Such renegotiations are called *conversion*.

What is conversion for us, women of the church at the end of the twentieth century? Conversion involves a turning toward God and away from all that blocks our relationship with God, ourselves, and the rest of creation. But the dynamics of conversion are not simply a process of looking in one direction and then deciding to turn and look in another. That image leaves us too much in control, too distanced and disengaged in some part of ourselves from what happens. It misses the depth, the wrenching that conversion involves.

Conversion is nothing less than being moved from one standpoint to another, literally shifted from occupying one space to occupying another. When a woman bears a child her standpoint changes. She is changed. The woman is now a mother and will never perceive and experience life quite as she did before. Times of birth, loss, or making lifelong commitments illustrate pointedly how our standpoints shift. When we are moved to a different place we are changed, we perceive life differently, and we act differently. We live a different story. Conversion remakes us in the core of our being. We cannot go back to who we were or act as we acted before we entered this new space and saw, felt, and experienced new things. Going back would violate the very essence of ourselves.

So, when we find ourselves "standing by the river, dying of thirst," our very survival depends on making a choice. If we stay where we are, we invite slow death. If we choose to walk away from our Christian tradition, we may very well find another path to God, the Living Water whom we seek. But if we find ourselves remaining, we may choose to stay in a different way, remaining by entering fully into our experience of dislocation and frustrated longing as an invitation to conversion. This invitation asks us to move toward God through all the reflection, questions, feelings, and decisions that are part of our process of renegotiation.

Both we and our tradition come out of such faithfully lived conversion experiences greatly changed. In faith, we hope that the changes lead us in the direction of a deeper and more intimate relationship with God. In faith, we hope that the changes will make the church a more vital and viable resource for women on their journey to God—for their sakes as well as the church's.

How to Renegotiate?

Few of us have been taught to think about relationships as something we negotiate. So the question—How does a woman renegotiate a relationship to her heritage in an authentic and faithful way?—may be startling. Realizing that on the journey of faith our relationship to a religious heritage must be renegotiated repeatedly may be even more surprising. Few of us have been taught that doubts and critical questions not only are valid and essential parts of our journeys in faith, but actually nurture faith by moving us more deeply into our lives and into our religious heritage. So, we are caught off guard and frequently do not know how to attend in a discerning way to the feelings and inner instincts that accompany such times of questioning. Few of us have been taught how to tap the images and themes of our Christian heritage as resources for imagination, for generating new options and perspectives at these times of transition and challenge in our lives.

This lack of teaching and practice about how to tap the resources of our tradition for wisdom and insight is particularly problematic today. It deprives us of the wisdom we need. It leaves us less able to discriminate among authentic and inauthentic ways to respond that our culture and religious communities offer us when we find our relationship to our religious heritage unsatisfying. Well-intentioned but inauthentic responses to our experience of frustrated longing are the paths of conformity or rebellion.[4]

Searching for Safety: Willed Conformity

Sometimes a woman, startled or frightened by the experience of frustrated desire and a sense of dislocation from her community, reacts by seeking safety, even salvation, through a willed effort to conform to the tradition as she has understood it. She appeals to her own will and the authority of the tradition to eliminate the frustration she feels. "Just believe more strongly and submit to the tradition and its leaders, who of course know better and more than you," she may tell herself. So she throws herself into intense involvement with many activities in a congregation or into extended prayer and practices of repentance for her lack of faith, all action aimed at subduing the pain of her longing and dislocation.

While her attempt may assuage the pain by virtue of sheer exhaustion and overactivity, this is not a permanent or finally satisfying solution. In fact, it is damaging to the woman and her spiritual growth because it denies the wisdom of her lived experience, turns an adult into a child, and transforms the Christian tradition and ecclesiastical structures into idols. A strongly willed faith and unquestioned submission to authority may leave a veneer of comfort in certitude and righteousness, as the strategy of willed conformity works temporarily. They may leave us quite confident that we know what God wants for us and what God expects other people to do. But when this surety fails, it leaves only deeper pain, exhaustion, disillusionment, and blind rage. For the strategy of conforming totally costs us our very selves and the pulsating, sometimes doubting, sometimes frightening, sometimes joy-saturated experience of a living faith. Total conformity precludes developing a mature relationship with God.

Creating Safety: Outright Rebellion

Opposite in ideological position but similar in structure is the path of relating to the tradition exclusively from the stance of outright rebellion. In this stance good advice, "Pay attention to your own experience and feelings," is revised to "Pay attention *only* to your own experience and feelings." So, we focus myopically on our own experiences and feelings to the exclusion of any outside factors. We experience, hear, and receive what our church teaches and does only from a stance of negative judgment. We expect nothing of value or insight to come from it. What does not match what we already think we automatically dismiss. Whether we remain in the tradition or leave it matters little, for we are defining ourselves almost exclusively in opposition to whatever our religious heritage has taught and what our denominational leadership has done.

The standpoint of rebellion often is a place of cleansing and of intensifying energy for a woman and so a constructive moment in her journey of faith. But if we remain forever in the standpoint of rebellion, in the end it leaves us focusing so intently on our own experience that anything else we encounter—other people's experience or a religious tradition—serves only as a mirror for our own thoughts and feelings. We cannot see anything besides ourselves; we understand nothing other in its own terms. Nothing is strange, new, or surprising. Anything that does not relate to our current experience and way of interpreting the world does not exist. We are caught in ourselves, a very tough place to be caught when it is a place of longing, dislocation, and frustration. These feelings can blind us, leaving us mired in cynicism and despair.

Remaining in outright rebellion to the Christian heritage blocks us from access to the deeper wisdom and meaning that a religious Wisdom tradition can disclose in our experience. Having been harmed by our tradition, we deny the possibility that the tradition might read our lives freshly in any way. We ground ourselves in a dignified, justice-insulted anger in order to insulate ourselves from further harm. But the cost of so steeling ourselves is never to be open to newness, to surprise, to grace.

Willed conformity and outright rebellion in the end are inadequate strategies for renegotiating our relationship with our Christian heritage. As final standpoints they are places of false conversion. Both mirror assumptions widely held in the United States: first, that we should join and participate only in groups where we can "agree" and "sign on" fully to what that group stands for, says, and does; and, second, that remaining with a group or organization when we experience internal dissonance is "hypocritical" at worst or neurotic at best. Neither stance is realistic. Together they reveal the extent to which perfectionism, individualism, and control dominate as highly valued goals in a culture permeated by fear.

Neither willed conformity nor outright rebellion finally serves the full development of human beings and communities. When we seek to mold our will, our feelings, and all our actions to some external norm that we believe will give us value, we destroy ourselves and our capacity to access the power of our religious heritage to nurture life. When we react to ideas, authorities, and practices from our Christian community only with suspicion and anger, we destroy ourselves by numbing our capacity to perceive aspects of our own inner lives. We also cut off the possibility of having our lives read in fresh ways by our Christian heritage. Willed conformity and outright rebellion each collapses a set of dynamic tensions that are essential to relationship: the dynamic tension between an individual and her experience; between an individual and her religious heritage; and between an individual and her community. Room for some tension and difference in all three is essential for a person to grow, for creativity to exist, for cultures to develop. The stances of willed conformity and outright rebellion shore up boundaries of a particular standpoint, leaving no room for newness—one of the biblical indications of God's presence. Neither, then, offers a way to renegotiate a *relationship* with our Christian heritage, because neither allows for mutuality, for newness, or for surprise.

Creative Engagement

There is another path to renegotiating our relationship to our Christian heritage, the path of creative engagement. On this path a woman turns to her heritage, expecting it to give her resources that can assist her as she encounters new situations in life. This way of relating involves a full range of human response and action in relation to her Christian tradition: being critical of it, being willing to face its limitations and sinfulness, rejecting its authority and rules in given situations and accepting them in others, being able to be carried by the tradition's resources and at the same time to act as prophet and critic. These ways of relating to the tradition may seem logically contradictory. However, they are the multidimensional response of a living, thinking individual who takes a tradition seriously. They are the response of a woman engaged by the tradition.

The path of creative engagement invites us to enter fully into our experience, trusting that God is with us in it. It asks us not to accept as the final truth the fear, anger, dryness, or disillusionment that come when we experience longing for God, frustration of that longing, and dislocation from our religious heritage. It invites us to explore our experience openly and fully in relationship to our Christian heritage, expecting creative inspiration for addressing the new challenges and situations that our lives present us. This strategy trusts that our experience and our Christian heritage each has a God-given integrity and that in their profoundest meaning they will not be mutually contradictory. It is grounded in the deep conviction that a woman's dislocations, dissatisfactions, judgments in contrast experiences, and desires are carriers of God's and her mutual longing. It is rooted in the intimate connection between a woman finding her own voice and learning to notice and honor the wisdom of her own faith. It searches out the dynamic tension between a woman's religious heritage and her particular experiences as the place where God's nourishing word is fully present to her, calling her to be a wise woman.

Creative engagement requires a woman to grow in her sense of her own authority and integrity. When a woman establishes or becomes aware of appropriate boundaries between herself, her community, and her religious tradition, she becomes more willing to act on her own thoughtful and informed integrity and less willing to act because of the insistence or expectations of others. She becomes more free and more responsible for her life and hence better able to cooperate with the movements of God's presence and grace in her life and in the world. Sr. Thea Bowman embodied this way of being as she sang and danced and told the story of

African-American Catholic Christians for all the church. The wide appeal of Joan Chittister's vision to women across the church today is grounded in her gift for bringing the power of the Christian heritage to women's lives.

Responding to deep but frustrated longing for God by creatively engaging the experience, a woman finds herself beckoned to befriend the Christian heritage as a rich Wisdom tradition. She finds herself drawn to tap that tradition as a source of both criticism and creative imagination in her life. The path of creative engagement leads a woman to trust that the experience of listening to her longing brings her to God, and that the resources of her Christian heritage can help. Women on this path trust that learning how to notice and mine the revelatory power of their own life experiences and putting them into conversation with the Christian heritage is the way that we begin to give voice to our faith. Learning to voice the faithful wisdom of our own life's journey is the way of wise faith.

⋐❦⋑

Pause for Reflection

1. The realization that her relationship to her religious tradition is dislocated, even conflicted, comes to a woman in different ways. Sometimes it comes through experiences of frustration. At other times it comes when voicing a prophetic "no" in a contrast experience. Some women realize their situation through the acknowledgment of a deep longing.

What brought you to the realization that you are "standing by a river, dying of thirst," that your Christian heritage is not nourishing you as you would like? What experience or series of experiences brought you to the point of recognizing your longing for God and your frustration with your Christian heritage?

Pick four adjectives that accurately describe that experience for you. Use the words to create a prayer or poem of your longing.

2. When have you found yourself responding to the situation of being unnourished by your Christian heritage either by willing stronger faith and submission or by being rebellious? What happened when you willed conformity? Describe. What happened when you entered and maintained a stance of rebellion toward your Christian tradition? Describe. Did either of these approaches lead to nourishment for you? Did either cover up your longing for God and for nourishment?

3. *At times, even if only for short moments, women are nourished by the Christian heritage. Recall a time when you felt fed by words or rituals or a community that were generated in some way by your association with the Christian tradition. Describe the event. What happened? What did you feel when the event began? How did you feel yourself being nourished? What does remembering this experience of sustenance do for you now?*

4. *The woman with the hemorrhage had a faith shaped by resistance and desire. Describe a time in your life when resistance and desire motivated you to care for yourself, to achieve a goal, to nurture a project or a person?*

5. *Reread the story of Lucy Burns. What attracts you in this story? How does this foremother's experiences of life and of faith resonate with your own? What does her story make you notice in your own? What does her story lead you to grieve in your own? What does her story lead you to hope for in your own?*

5

The Power of Voice

⌘

To Speak at the Water's Edge

Hope-filled but frustrated longing for God—the experience of a woman who is "standing by a river, dying of thirst." It hardly seems a space of giftedness, yet that it precisely what it can become. Through dislocation, dissatisfaction, contrast experience, or desire, a woman becomes aware of herself, of her thoughts and feelings about her situation and her relationship to her Christian tradition, and begins to shape and utter her reflections. At first she may be aware only of intense feelings of sorrow or anger or fear. Then she may move on to form preliminary statements about the events and situations that contribute to her feelings. Later, she may articulate her own position about what she thinks is true, right, good, just, or faithful about particular issues in her life, in her parish, or in the church. Sometimes a woman speaks her feelings and reflections only to herself in her musings or by writing in a journal. Sometimes she voices them tentatively to a friend or a group of trusted women. Her ability and willingness to move from awareness of her feelings to articulating her reflections depends much on her context and on how others respond to her. But wherever a woman is in this process, she has begun to find her own voice. Finding her voice, befriending herself—this is the surprising gift that "standing by a river dying of thirst" can bring.

Some of us first discover our voices through that experience. Others find their voices strengthened, deepened, and challenged.

Either way, a woman is invited to take a crucial step in accepting the invitation to renegotiate her relationship to the Christian tradition. It is a negative step, a "no" that can stand for all the "no's" a woman did not or could not say in her life; it is a choice to refrain from devaluing and discounting her own voice.[1]

This is not an easy step. Few women have been raised to reverence themselves or the insights, questions, and observations they might be moved to speak. Reaching this point of self-awareness, self-affirmation, and self-valuing is both gift and achievement for us and often difficult. It is difficult because of problems in the ways that women are socialized in our society and the ways that socialization is reinforced and supported by Christian denominations. Women still are worth less economically, receive less education, and occupy fewer positions of power and influence in business, politics, human services, education, and the arts than do men. We still suffer from discrimination, dehumanization, and danger justified by religious and cultural teachings that bolster androcentric and patriarchal worlds. And more women than men are poor in the United States and around the world.[2]

For some women, recognizing our inferior status as women is a very painful part of our awakening. But this painful realization often constitutes the first step in becoming aware of and beginning to analyze the situation of women in society. However distressing and uncomfortable it may be, it is also freeing. It moves a woman from thinking that she alone is individually responsible for her plight and isolated in it, to recognizing the complex relationships and structures that shape individuals and society. For example, "no fault divorce" sounds great, but it usually leaves women and children with inadequate economic resources. Similarly, one might consider admirable the goal of instilling "personal responsibility" into people deprived of it by dependence on welfare. But focus on this individual value obscures our seeing the ways that our economic system creates and actually requires a permanent class of unemployed and underemployed persons in order to operate. Only when we begin to see our problems in larger contexts and stop taking unlimited responsibility for every dimension of our life situation are we freed to act in more creative ways to find solutions to our problems.

Understanding the place of women in society and in the church, then, is inextricably linked to the way a woman's faith develops when she finds herself "standing by the river, dying of thirst." The ability to put what is happening to her into a larger context, the ability to name her feelings and thoughts *even when persons in authority have labeled them forbidden* are crucial to her maturity and integrity. Very simply, a woman cannot move from standing by the river to drinking from it without discovering her own voice. Once she has begun to do so, she cannot walk back into ignorance or naiveté or ever again be anonymous to herself. Instead, she must begin to understand all that "voice" implies.

The Power of Voice

To have a voice, to have the ability to speak what one thinks and feels is a powerful thing. Ancient cultures understood much better than we in our sound-saturated world the power of voice. We need their perception to grasp the import of the book of Genesis when it tells us that God creates by the power of the word, by voicing the intention to create. In John's gospel Jesus is presented as the *Logos*, the *Word* of God, through whom all things were created. Speaking an intention or a desire or a feeling or a judgment creates reality and reconfigures existence. In our word-glutted world we too often are unaware of this power and numb to its results.

Think about voices you have heard: voices that spoke truth to you and that told lies; voices that concealed important information or feelings from you; voices that revealed for you insight and love; voices that charmed and enthralled you with stories or songs; voices that comforted you in times of trouble; voices that ridiculed or demeaned or dismissed or cut you to the quick or in other ways assaulted you; and voices that invited you to new confidence, new actions, new ways of being your best self. In myriad ways all these voices shaped you, enriching and diminishing, constraining and evoking your thoughts, actions, and sense of yourself.

Think about the quality of voices you have heard: soft and loud, cynical and hopeful, tired and energetic, frightened and angry, choked and resonant. The tone and quality of voices convey messages too: acceptance or disapproval, confidence or anxiety, safety or threat. Sometimes that message is intended for the hearer. Sometimes it reveals much more the world that the speaker inhabits, the speaker's experience of reality.

Think too about those who have no voice, those who out of fear or illness or abuse or spiritual malaise or economic and political and racial and gender oppression are silent. How many women do not speak in voices loud enough to be heard? Voice is powerful in its presence and in its absence, in what is spoken and in what is not spoken, in the tones of sound and of silence.

Voice captures perhaps better than any other image the relational quality of existence. The scriptures are full of the word, each reference connected to relationship and communication with God, between God and people, or among people: "harkening to God's voice," "raising voices," "crying out in a loud voice," recognizing a "still, small voice." "Voice" appears nearly five hundred times in the Bible, as a verb and as a noun. "Word" appears over ten thousand times.

Voice assumes individuals in relationship—speakers and listeners whose interaction shapes each person and community, selves whose intentions and actions have consequences far beyond themselves. Voice conveys the participatory and relational character of life. Cruel voices chill to the bone because they convey a deliberate desire to breach relationship. Voices expressing grief and abandonment evoke sorrow in listeners, again because they convey so powerfully the pain of broken relationships. When we pay attention to voices, the medium of expression that most fully conveys embodied thought and feeling, we are forced to acknowledge our fundamental interdependence. When we pay attention to voices we begin to perceive how deeply dialogue and interaction shape individuals, cultures, and worlds, how they shape truth and meaning in human life. This way of perceiving truth and meaning and reality stands in stark contrast to the more common view in Western cultures during the modern period: a distanced, disconnected, dispassionate observer seeing what is "out there."[3]

In the Jewish and Christian traditions, "harkening to God's voice" and responding to God with one's voice, a voice saturated with the full dimensions of feeling that one has at the moment, are intimately connected to knowing Wisdom and becoming wise.

> Wisdom cries out in the street;
>   in the squares she raises her voice.
> At the busiest corner she cries out;
>   at the entrance of the city gates she speaks.
>   (Prv 1:20–21).

Wisdom cries out to the people, asking them to pay attention to what she teaches. She cries out because she desires the people's welfare. In Jewish Scriptures, Wisdom is the desiring, often feminine image of God, a God longing for God's people. Wisdom cries out to the people because she wants them to learn how to live in relationship to God, self, neighbor, and earth so that there is peace and sufficiency for all.[4]

But desiring must be a two-way street if this world of peace and sufficiency for all is to exist. Persons must desire Wisdom as much as she desires them, and they must cry out in return. Wisdom says,

> If you accept my words and treasure up my
>   commandments within you,
> making your ear attentive to wisdom
>   and inclining your heart to
>   understanding,
> if you indeed cry out for insight
>   and raise your voice for understanding
>   (Prv 2:1–3)

then you will know God and be able to discern the path of faithfulness in your life. The scriptures are clear; we must desire Wisdom to find it, we must

> seek it like silver,
>   and search for it as for hidden treasures.
>   (Prv 2:4)

Wisdom is both gift and fulfillment of our desire for God and for fullness of life. But we cannot receive this gift, cannot hear Wisdom's desire for us, and cannot respond to it unless we find and befriend our own voices.

Voices, Selves, and Contexts

Thinking about how our own voices develop provides us access to how we have come to be the persons we are. It focuses our attention on the biological, social, cultural, and spiritual forces that shape us.

Certain things about our voices are inherited genetically: pitch, range of tone, even volume capacity. But physical capacity is a small part of what constitutes our voices. When, whether, and how we use our voices depends much more on our experiences in relationships, family, social class, culture, and the larger society. Many women remember keenly being told as they moved from childhood into adolescence: "Don't talk so loudly; it isn't ladylike." Many women remember meals where men spoke at the table and where women were, like children, seen and not heard. Women have been and still are beaten, belittled, or in other ways punished for speaking at all.

Often, unbeknown to us, the tones of our voices carry our entire autobiographies. This realization might dawn in us when we stand in a supermarket line or sit in a doctor's waiting room. Which of us in these and similar situations has not heard a whole life of pain or joy or sorrow expressed in the voices of anonymous women around us as they spoke to children or nurses or clerks? Our voices carry the joy, sadness, anger, fear, concerns, and frustration of our lives.

Feminist writers have been attending to the relationship between the development of women's voices and selves for thirty years now. Works using the image of gaining voice to talk about women's development began appearing in the 1970s. Tillie Olsen's *Silences* (1978) explores obstacles to creativity and looks pointedly at why we have the silence rather than the words of so many women writers. She locates the answer in women's social situations, the fact that they spend so much of their lives caring for others, putting their own creative projects second. Olsen's own short stories convey eloquently the situation of women in webs of caring relationships. "I Stand Here Ironing" is a poignant presentation of a mother's concern for her adolescent daughter that is at the same time a whispered lament for her own life.[5] Carol Gilligan's *In A Different Voice* (1982) carefully describes the differences in how women and men make moral decisions. She argues that in spite of theories to the contrary, women are not inherently less mature than men because women, in working with difficult situations, tend to think about how the situation looks from the perspective of all those involved and to seek solutions that meet the needs of as many as possible. Her work is important for forcing researchers to factor the nature and character of relationships into their studies of moral and cognitive development.[6] In 1986

Mary Field Belenky, Blythe McVicker Clinchy, Nancy Rule Gold-berger, and Jill Mattuck Tarule in *Women's Ways of Knowing* helped make voice a dominant metaphor for understanding how women develop a sense of themselves, their agency, and their possible contributions to their worlds. The *Women's Ways of Knowing* Collective explored women's cognitive, psychological, and emotional development through intense interviews with over one hundred and thirty women from very different ethnic, economic class, and educational backgrounds. The women they interviewed used the image "gaining a voice" more than any other to describe their own processes of growth and change.[7]

In *Women's Ways of Knowing* the authors describe different forms of voice that women may have at different periods in their lives. Voice includes a woman's sense of self and her cognitive and emotional processes. They place women's voices in a series that is successively rich. These forms of voice range from voicelessness— a state of being isolated, passive, reactive, dependent on authorities seen as all-powerful, a state of being unaware of self or center—to fully developed, integrated voice. Between voicelessness and fully developed voice is a spectrum of voices through which women may move: received voice, where women accept and repeat what authorities say; inner voice, where women come to trust their own intuition and judgment most of all; and the voice of reason, where women adopt the procedural language of a particular discipline.[8]

Olsen, Gilligan, the *Women's Ways of Knowing* Collective, and other feminist writers, researchers, and therapists explore different dimensions of women's lives and development using the image of voice to focus their effort to understand how a woman comes to, develops, and sustains a sense of herself within the network of relationships and care-giving responsibilities that shape women's lives.[9] Their work is very important for showing how profoundly relationships constitute the context of a woman's development. So much is this the case that anthropologist Mary Catherine Bateson has studied how women put their lives together improvisationally, creating and nurturing projects of their own amid constantly changing circumstances—often around the margins of their spouses' careers and children's needs and punctuated by the rhythms of interruption and delay. Women who succeed in imagining and bringing their own creative projects to life often do so by coupling tenacity and passion with a capacity to see unrecognized possibilities in what others consider leftovers and crumbs.[10]

Developing Our Voices[11]

A woman's voice develops as she grows and matures in interaction with herself and her world. The care she receives as an infant and child from primary caregivers, usually especially her mother, is fundamental to her capacity to develop a voice.[12] A child needs unconditional positive regard and love to begin to develop her voice. She needs to receive the message that it is all right for her to feel what she feels and to express it. Girls who are punished and criticized repeatedly for expressing their feelings, for saying "no," for being uncooperative and unhelpful do not develop strong and clear voices. A girl needs to be asked what she thinks and to have what she says be heard and respected. Too often, however, girls are not asked and neither are their mothers, so they grow up unaware of their own thinking. Girls who suffer sexual abuse are even less likely to develop a healthy sense of self or a voice.

Unless they receive help to remedy the abuse and lack of care in their early childhood, women who grow up in these circumstances generally end up voiceless. While they may be aware of intense feelings of pain or fear or desire, they have no way to make sense of these feelings. They know them only as dangerous. They do not know how to move from the experience of desire to forming a goal, and then to realizing it. They have not developed a capacity for self-transcendence, a capacity to reflect on one's self and one's experience. Such women have difficulty identifying patterns in their own behavior or in how others act toward them. They are not able to imagine life empathetically from the perspective of another. As a result, they do not know how to construct or discern meaning in their lives. They experience their lives as capricious and dangerous and generally full of pain.[13]

Even women less crippled by their upbringing know the experience of voicelessness. The image of screaming at the top of her lungs while surrounded by a crowd of people, but isolated and unnoticed in a clear but soundproof container, is one I have heard frequently in groups of women speaking about their life journeys. Invisibility is frustrating, demeaning, heartbreaking. A daily life filled with small experiences of not being heard or of having what she says dismissed, debilitates, and eats at the soul of a woman. Voicelessness destroys her spirit.

Whether and how a girl is encouraged to think and to speak can even affect the quality of her voice physically. Christin Lore Weber tells a story in her book *Womanchrist* about teaching speech and drama to a group of novices at a convent in the Midwest. She described her biggest challenge as *helping them find their voices*. Though all the women were adults in their early twenties, they had the voices of small girls. Lore worked with these young women to help them find their body's center so they could find the source of their voices. At the end of the summer the novices' voices were different, much stronger and more assured. Equally significant, the novices themselves were different, far less submissive and dependent, and far more in touch with their own power.[14]

Women who as infants and little girls escape the forces that would leave them voiceless begin to exercise their own voices by accepting what their parents and other authorities tell them.[15] This is a normal developmental stage, one where children and young adults tend to be dualistic. They see the world as black and white, good and bad, with good defined by what one's parents or other authorities think and bad defined as that which is different. In this stage girls and young women repeat what they have heard from authorities whom they trust. This is how they make meaning in their lives. Any idea or situation that challenges what the authorities have said is dangerous. As girls grow into young women and expand their knowledge and sets of relationships, the frequency of dangerous encounters increases. How they negotiate these encounters influences greatly the kind of voice they develop as adult women. Whether they can negotiate them depends significantly on supportive parents or other adult figures who create a space within which girls can exercise independent thought.

The issues that constitute dangerous encounters need not be large. In one group a woman told about the intense feelings of betrayal she felt when she admitted to herself that she liked irises. Her mother had "hated irises" she said, always cutting them down, never letting them bloom. The woman knew now that her mother's actions were motivated by her severe sinus problems. The irises aggravated her very debilitating condition. Even knowing this, the woman who shared the story still felt deeply the dangerous betrayal that came with independent thought. Especially for women, who learn very early that to displease others, to put oneself and one's desires ahead of others, is to court abandonment and death, independent thought is dangerous indeed. Many women do not move beyond the point of mirroring and repeating what the external authorities say, whether that authority is parent, husband, or church. Such women invest much in making the world conform to their/the authorities' view.

The inner conflict and sense of danger is so intense for many women that if they do begin to think independently, to develop a voice uniquely their own, they seek another way to resolve the tension of independent thinking while being in relationship. They move from trusting external authorities to trusting only themselves. Women may make this move from late adolescence to mid-adulthood, if they make it at all. Such women turn to their own intuition, their own inner sense, as the most trustworthy guide to life.[16] Women guided by this inner voice take control of their own lives. They do act independently, often beginning to nurture their own dreams and creative projects with some sustained care. Yet women enthralled with the authority and power of their own inner voice may rely too heavily on this one source and find themselves cut off from other sources of authority and insight that might be useful in their lives. Still another danger is the temptation to avoid the tension of thinking independently while in relationship.

As women mature, another possibility becomes open to some of them, the possibility of mastering the procedural and technical discourse that is part of a particular discipline or field. Learning a methodological discourse gives women access to a community of voices focused around a particular topic or set of problems. Women who are attracted to this more public way of speaking usually have sensed the limitations of isolated intuition and want more. But the power of procedural knowledge, the capacity to argue, make points, have one's position on a topic or plan prevail, can also be limiting. It can lead a woman to forget all the dimensions of her self and her life outside that particular procedural discourse.[17] Even more, a woman enamored of procedural knowledge may find herself acquiescing to total relativism. Knowing that each person speaks from a particular perspective, she may avoid the tension of asking how those perspectives interrelate or how all are related to her own values.

So far the picture of women's development of voice moves through a pattern of polarizations where self is one pole and other is the second pole: from voicelessness to received voice, then from inner voice to voice defined by the method of a profession such as law or business. One end of the pole is a more isolated self, the other end is a more external, public authority. Women may move from one extreme on the pole to the other and back again.

But if a woman is fortunate enough to have been given the resources and support to develop fully, she may reach a place that is more integrated, that can take account of both ends of the polarity at the same time. These are the women who develop what the *Women's Ways of Knowing* Collective calls *"integrated voice."*[18] A woman at this stage of development can negotiate the tensions of thinking and feeling for herself while in relationships that matter deeply to her. Such women are articulate and reflective. They notice and care about their own and others' lives and inner processes. They are aware of their own thoughts, judgments, moods, and desires. They weave together rational and emotive thought. They can integrate disciplinary knowledge about external realities and their own inner knowledge and intuitions about people, relationships, and situations. These women are invested in genuine conversation about things that matter to them. They speak compassionately and intelligently from a centered, relational self.

Women of integrated voice have learned to relate to themselves and their worlds in creative ways. They have learned how to notice and draw upon their feelings, their embodied, holistic response to life as a resource.[19] These women have negotiated experiences of disappointment and disillusionment and come out wiser and more perceptive. They know how to dream and how to bring dreams to reality. They also know how to grieve their losses.

Given the obstacles that women face in their lives—from being identified as disappointments to their fathers or mothers because they are female to the lifelong psychological, political, social, and economic consequences of patriarchy and sexism—it is understandable that not all develop full, strong, integrated voices. It is a waste that not all women have access to their own experience and creativity or to the resources that would allow them to develop into full, creative human beings.

Still, women do grow and change. They move among forms of voice at different times in their lives. While that movement does not always progress in a single direction, as women develop they tend not to return permanently to a more isolated form of voice.

Women's Voices and Their Religious Heritage

Women are in different places of development of voice. The place in which they stand at any given point in their lives shapes significantly whether and how they may undertake renegotiating their relationship with their religious heritage.[20]

It is impossible for a voiceless woman to renegotiate her relationships to the people around her, let alone her religious tradition. Her experiences of abuse and her fear of punishment make it impossible for her to criticize her situation in a sustained manner. The contrast between what is and what might be escapes her. A woman in this place is not secure enough and often not physically safe enough to be able to endure the dissonance that is part of a path to a new relationship with one's religious tradition. If such a woman is connected to the Christian tradition in particular, she most likely experiences it as sanctioning the abuse and punishment that she receives at the hands of family and institutions.

Working out of an almost overpowering desire for self-survival, religious institutions and their leaders want women (and men) to remain in the place where they accept what the authorities say. Institutions feel more comfortable with members who are meek, obedient, and adoring. In the Roman Catholic Church in the United States, when *Humanae Vitae* was promulgated, the Vatican expected people to oblige unquestioningly. When the Vatican proclaimed recently that the topic of women's ordination could no longer be discussed, it expected an acquiescing response from laity in the church: the ending of all discussion on the topic because church members would automatically trust that it is best to do as the authority instructs, for those in authority know better. Not having achieved their desired response, the Vatican raised the ante on its authority by ascribing a theologically and historically unprecedented kind of infallibility to the teaching that women cannot be ordained. Such unwarranted exercise of authority undermines the credibility of the church among those who have moved beyond merely accepting what authorities say.

Accepting what the authorities say becomes a comical parody when a woman remains in this place throughout her adult life. Yet, this stance is appropriate at a certain point in her development. When she was a young child, her willingness to accept authoritative teachings helped her to learn a good deal about her religious tradition. She assumed that her religious tradition, like her parents and teachers, had something to offer her—indeed, that her religious tradition was essential to what matters most in a woman's life.

Women who have remained in the place of repeating what authorities say should not be denigrated for not having moved toward more independent thinking. The trust in their religious heritage that undergirds their repetition can be a resource for them. Often the tradition's words and symbols comfort and support women in extremely difficult situations where they judge that they have no other options than to endure. For example, Catholic women's devotion to St. Jude Thaddeus, patron of impossible cases, helped a generation of women born of immigrant parents to negotiate the shifting social roles and responsibilities required of them as their families became acculturated in the United States.[21] A tradition can create zones of psychic and spiritual freedom in situations where social, economic, and political freedom are remote possibilities, if possible at all.[22]

Women in this stage of development, which the *Women's Ways of Knowing* Collective calls the place of "received voice," value their religious tradition very highly, sometimes to the point of idolizing it. Because they understand the church to be totally good, they cannot conceive that the authorities in the church could do harm to women or that they could make mistakes. These women often experience intense disillusionment when authority figures behave in such blatantly abusive or inappropriate ways that reality can no longer be ignored; for example, when a pastoral leader acts in sexually inappropriate ways. Their disillusionment is frightening to them because, occupying a black-and-white world, they encounter only emptiness once they see that the church is flawed.

This is a very painful experience. What one has experienced as nurturing may now be poisoning. Sometimes women do not know how to move from this place of pain. Leaving the church or repressing their own thoughts and feelings may seem the only options. The former may lead a particular woman to the path of religious growth in another setting. If her disillusionment has undercut entirely the credibility of her religious heritage or community, this may be the only appropriate path for her and a far healthier path than repressing her experience. Yet abandoning her religious heritage can leave a woman adrift with no tradition of spiritual resources to support her development. Drifting also can kill the human spirit. Repressing one's own thoughts and feelings as unacceptable will surely do so.

The tradition's words and symbols can support a woman to find a path other than repressing her own thoughts and feelings or leaving her church. Often situations of pain create an altered spiritual and psychological space where familiar symbols and images generate surprising new ideas and possibilities. This is part of the power of religious traditions: their symbols subvert structures and situations as easily as they create and reinforce them. Because symbols are never exhausted by the interpretations made of them by the people with power, symbols can stimulate imagination, warrant resistance to oppression, and provide a critical angle of vision that a woman can use to reassess her situation. Symbols can become a school of discriminating perception for those who will spend time with them.

Women who have moved from uncritically accepting the teachings of external authorities to the place of relying on their own intuition and inner perceptions often are very interested in women's wisdom and in the special way that women can know. As the twentieth century draws to an end, many women in the church find themselves moving toward or being pushed toward this place of "inner voice."[23] These women see very clearly the foibles and fallibility of the institutional church. Many have known intensely the hope-filled and frustrated longing of "standing by the river, dying of thirst." They increasingly assume that in light of the massive androcentrism and patriarchy of Christian churches, their theological and spiritual heritage has little to offer women.

Some of these women remain in the church because of smaller supportive communities rooted in a particular parish or because remaining generates less conflict in the family system than leaving. They may affiliate with a particular parish because it meets their needs but feel little if any connection to the historical tradition of Christianity. Disillusioned in the past and frequently disappointed with much in the church in the present, these women turn to their own inner wisdom and resources as the only reliable guides to nourishing their spiritual hunger. It may make sense for them to abandon the Christian heritage as a resource for women. It may become opaque for them, and in an effort to survive, some dismiss the pain of not being fed by their own tradition.

The danger for women in this stage is to become casual consumers of spiritual Wisdom traditions. For a Wisdom tradition to ground significant critique of her life and to fund creative imagination, a woman must take it seriously, spend time with it, be willing to reflect on her life through it. This kind of relationship is not developed through casual contact with the teachings or practices of a tradition. Some women turn to women's spirituality movements, often influenced by transformational psychology, Native American traditions, or an eclectic New Age collage of ideas and practices, or to the religious traditions of long-dead matriarchal societies for spiritual resources outside themselves. While exploring women's wisdom from across cultures can be affirming for women and helpful because it provides comparative perspective, sooner or later a woman must ground herself sufficiently in a tradition for it to become a genuine conversation partner. Any tradition, like any friend, spouse, or community, is not perfect. The path to spiritual maturity requires women to recognize the imperfection of their Wisdom tradition—Christian, goddess, or other—and then to decide whether or not to claim it as their own. Such a choice, made by a woman who takes responsibility for her own life, is crucial to maturing faith.

Rather than move into the wisdom of women, some Christian women seek to feed their hope-filled longing through study, by entering the discourse communities of theology and church history. They might study the history of women mystics and read theology written by contemporary feminist theologians. Some seek formal education in theology, scripture, and ministry as a route to connecting to the rich resources of their Christian heritage. While these women still hold the conviction that their Christian heritage has something to offer, they approach the tradition from a critical, analytical perspective. Completing formal study and training can, however, lead to new experiences of frustrated longing and dislocation in relation to their religious heritage. Well-trained women with degrees often are not hired into parish or diocesan positions. Such women are replaced by less qualified candidates, or are not allowed to preach, or are forbidden public roles and given only private ones, or have their work dismantled, or have credit for their work taken by the pastor, and the list goes on.

This is a painful way to be "standing by the river, dying of thirst," especially if one pursued education as a route to legitimacy in the institutional structures of the church. Anger may consume women in this place, who find themselves bitterly disappointed by what they cannot do in the church and deeply hurt by the nonrecognition of their expertise and skill in theological and ministerial disciplines. Many find that they must leave their denomination or the Christian tradition entirely.

The challenge that comes to women in this situation is to face the harsh reality of sin in the structures of the church. To be able to drink from the river without the water tasting like the gall of bitterness, women here must gain a new existential appreciation of solidarity in sin and grace. Often this comes as women glimpse the powerful workings of God's Spirit in multiple dimensions of church and society. The glimpse of God's movement beyond institutional bounds can free such women from desire for recognition and sanction from the institutional fathers. Negotiating this movement is not easy and is often complex. Women support and nurture other women into this space. Their mutual support is crucial because they are noticing and building an alternative reality, one that contradicts what the massive institutional structure represents. Grounded in this alternative reality, these women can pronounce the prophetic "no" to the institutional church more congruently than before and with less damage to themselves.

Some women reach a place of "integrated voice" in relation to their religious tradition and community. All who speak in this voice have moved through disappointment and disillusionment and found themselves grounded in their tradition at a deeper level. Often it is the women in parishes, especially women who have lived long, who know the most on this score, though frequently they are reluctant to voice their wisdom. However, when they tell stories of their own growing up in the church or of how they look at things, the depth of their insight and their ability to weave together seemingly contradictory aspects of their Christian heritage become evident. These women tell stories of growing and developing, coming to understand through episodes of their lives the inadequacy of the way they related to themselves and their religious traditions previously. Each woman of integrated voice found a path to a more adequate relationship with both.

Even for women who have strong, focused, integrated voices, there is a cost to being in relationship to their Christian heritage, a cost known in the pain of loneliness. The oppression they experience and of which they are keenly aware, the grinding weight of the patriarchal institution, the obvious invisibility that they live repeatedly in contacts with institutional religious authorities— these create their own kind of loneliness. There is another loneliness, though, the loneliness that is experienced in the desire for companions who share their vision and their joy. It is the loneliness of grief for their sisters who have not found a path to a renegotiated and life-giving relationship to their Christian heritage.

Understanding and appreciating the range of voices that are part of our individual and corporate lives as women are important to us as women of faith. We can listen to ourselves and to each other differently, with more nuanced awareness of the temptations and possibilities we confront. We can hold ourselves and our sisters with more compassion when we recognize that women experience themselves at odds with their Christian heritage for different reasons and in different ways at different times in their lives.

Moving Toward Full Voice

How do we move from one voice to another? This question is crucial from the perspective of women's spiritual growth. Psychological studies suggest that growth comes in several ways: the desire to care for another, usually a child, but sometimes a parent, friend, husband, partner, or community; the mentoring of a caring friend or authority; and experiences of insight or beauty propel women on the journey toward integrated voice.[24] These clues suggest the relational quality of interactions that lead women to growth. They also suggest that each of these experiences disrupts a woman's world and forces reinterpretation of herself, her situation, her purposes in life.

The kinds of situations that psychologists describe as motivating movement from one form of voice to another are those that the Christian tradition has taught lead humans to encounters with Mystery, with God. This tradition from ascetical theology flies in the face of some popular contemporary Christian understandings in the United States, understandings that suggest a God who only reinforces and supports social, economic, and professional success, and understandings that view pain and loss in life solely as punishment. Still, the older spiritual tradition invites a person of faith to await the invitation to new relationship in any crisis situation.

The Christian heritage always has understood that people become aware of God at key moments in their lives. Certain kinds of experiences are pregnant with Mystery inviting persons into relationship. This knowledge is part of the Catholic emphasis on sacraments. But while God's presence is powerful in particular ways through the formal sacraments, individuals have equally powerful, revealing experiences of Divine Mystery through events in their lives quite unconnected to the institutional church.

Certain kinds of experiences characteristically invite the encounter with Divine Mystery.[25] Experiences of contingency, communion, moral ambiguity, collapse, disenchantment, humor, play, freedom, and courage all allude to the Divine Mystery.

Experiences of contingency, where we come to reflect on the fact that our existence is given, unchosen, and will end, invite us to ponder the Mystery that is the context of our lives. When we bury a valued colleague who is struck down in only a few months from cancer or lose a friend in a freak accident, the contingency of our existence becomes pointedly clear.

Communion is another experience that exposes Divine Mystery. We know communion through powerful experiences in a family or prayer group or project group where we find ourselves energized, loved, supported, thriving. Experiences of communion make us keenly aware that we are bound to others by something that transcends, grounds, and enlivens us, but that we do not control. Experiences of communion lead us to savor the giftedness of our lives.

Experiences of moral ambiguity force us to face how intractable and inextricably bound together are both brokenness and healing in our individual lives and in all of human life. The need to feed her children may make a woman reluctant to report her supervisor's harassment. The desire to maintain academic standards may lead a teacher to give a student a lower mark despite her tremendous effort and great improvement over the semester. A pregnant woman's knowledge that the fetus she carries is deformed may lead her to choose abortion. In all these situations brokenness and healing, good and bad are intimately and complexly intertwined.

In experiences of collapse our bodies, minds, or spirits betray us, or ideas we have long cherished turn to straw—in whatever ways, our worlds fall apart. We age, and arthritis takes away our ability to draw, an ability that has been a source of admiration from others in our community and a source of worth to ourselves. A school where we have served as principal for many years is closed by the diocese or school district and cherished programs cease to exist.

Experiences of disenchantment confront us with the fact that an individual or a belief or a commitment or an institution or a relationship that we have valued, perhaps too highly, is not ultimate, is not God. The spouse we have loved and for whom we gave up our career proves unfaithful. Someone we thought was a friend turns away from us. We have been a loyal employee for years and then the company lays us off at age fifty-nine because we have become expendable. A religious community will not support a new ministry to which a woman who has given much to the community feels called.

Experiences of humor, filled with laughter and irony, reveal that each one can hold herself and her situation lightly because she is held by something bigger than herself. We laugh with delight as we tumble in autumn leaves with children or friends, becoming aware in an instant of how much our overly serious stance toward life costs us. Or we cry over a seemingly impossible task and then laughingly accept the ability to do only what we can do.

In play, delight refreshes and renews and we return from a time of self-transcendence holding ourselves and others more gently. Whether we have hiked or sewed or danced or kayaked, we have moved outside of ourselves for a while and come back more willing to be who we are, more accepting of our lives, more capable of loving.

Experiences of freedom, emblematic in situations of choice, lead us to reflect that, whatever our decisions, we choose consequences that we cannot predict, we choose lives that, in the end, we do not control. A twenty-fifth anniversary of marriage or religious life invites us to choose once again, in freedom, the life we chose once before. We say "yes" to a new professional opportunity that will move us halfway across a continent, away from friends, to a new challenge.

Finally, when we act with courage or see others act with courage, we become aware that our very lives and their meaning are captured in the capacity to risk loss of ourselves and our status for the care of others, for justice, for dignity, for ourselves. The capacity to act with courage even against impossible odds fascinates us. The stories of Anne Frank, Etty Hillesum, Corrie Ten Boom, Ita Ford, and other women capture our attention because they *lived* in impossible situations and acted in profoundly humane ways.[26] The popularity of stories about individuals who struggled against great odds and even lost their lives as a consequence of their courage and mission suggests the hunger in our world to know the source of that courage.[27]

All these experiences—contingency, communion, moral ambiguity, collapse, disenchantment, humor, play, freedom, and courage—share a common transformative moment. In this moment, whether short or long, a woman becomes intensely aware of herself and her life. For a brief time, and sometimes not until after intense pain, she views her life or experiences it in a way that feels far more real, rich, and full than the day-to-day existence she has known up to now. These encounters with Mystery nurture vision and hope. They may lead her to focus resources, courage, and commitment over time to enflesh that vision, to make it real.

The kinds of experiences that can lead a woman from one form of voice to another, then, are experiences that invite an encounter with Mystery. This means that a woman's movement from voicelessness to integrated or fully authentic voice is intimately connected to a woman's faith formation. Identifying patterns in the process of gaining voice and nurturing women through the process are important pastoral tasks. Once this is recognized, questions about how a religious tradition helps or hampers a woman's growth in voice become vital spiritual questions.

Authentic Voice

Because voice is so important for a women's psychological, cognitive, and spiritual development, the authenticity or inauthenticity of voices emerges as an important consideration. Which voices are true? Which are false or self-deceptive? How does a woman learn to listen and discern the authenticity of her own voice or other voices? What does it mean to have an authentic voice?

Feminist writers who focus on women's development describe authentic voice this way: To have an authentic voice means being able to locate ourselves in relation to our inner processes and our social and intellectual world. It means the capacity to name what we know, to speak out about it, and even to write about it. It means to be able to say to ourselves, "What do I think? What am I feeling? What do I have to say?" and to get answers from ourselves. To have authentic voice means to think about what we feel and to feel about what we think. To have authentic voice is to be aware of, comfortable with, and capable of expressing our center, mind, and feelings. It means being able to experience and acknowledge the full range of human feelings.

A woman of authentic voice can articulate her own particular wisdom and truth and relate it to the wisdom and truth of her religious tradition, her culture, and her world. She appreciates that each individual has unique experiences and perspectives, both convergent and divergent from those of others. She can speak her truth without needing it to be the only truth. Her self, her voice, and her mind have developed together.[28]

A significant dimension of authentic voice is the ability to resist. Women of authentic voice resist and disbelieve people, ideas, social systems, and the parts of themselves that say that women are lesser beings, of no value, unable, undesirable, unredeemable, unworthy, unlovable. Women of authentic voice recognize and accept the times and places where they have been complicit in their victimization by not speaking their truth to a church and a world so desperately in need of wisdom because it was easier to remain silent. Having learned to breathe in life deeply and to speak in words and acts the grace that they are, women of authentic voice have compassion for themselves and for others.

This description of authentic voice presents an idealized picture. Few women approach authentic voice in all parts of their lives all the time. The circumstances of women in our society make this nearly impossible. Still, women of authentic voice are in our lives, if we will but notice them. These are women who speak and act in ways that lead to life for themselves and for others. These women do not cower in the face of opposition. They demonstrate remarkable resilience. One finds such voice in Lucy Burns, Dorothy Day, and the other women who endured arrest and imprisonment because they believed women's full dignity as human beings entailed their having the vote. One finds it too in the mothers of the "disappeared" in Argentina who marched silently with placards picturing their children who had been arrested in the night. Women of authentic voice are grounded in a vision that allows them to be creative, compassionate, and committed to a range of projects and relationships.

We respond to women who do speak with authentic voices, and our response can be complex. Depending on where we are in our own development, we may respond to them with fascination or fear.[29] Either way, they have awakened us. What path will we travel once we have been awakened? The way these women are able to act, their courage, their vision, and their creativity may inspire us. We become fascinated by them and want to be able to live as they do, with a grace and freedom that is deeply rooted in their spirits. Their words and lives can energize and stimulate our own imaginations, offering concrete evidence that the promise of full life for us is not an empty promise. They become inspirations and symbols of hope as we seek to experience the deepest dimensions of reality with which they are in contact.

Women of authentic voice can evoke another response, though, a fear that quickly disguises itself as envy and harsh judgment. We may spiral into discouragement when we try to live as these women do and find out that it is not easy. Or we may be frightened by the challenges these women present to us in our own lives. When this happens we are inclined to criticize them, dismiss them, or question their faithfulness, integrity, and motivations; nearly any cover will do in order to avoid the hard questions these women's lives raise for us. So we hear that Mother Teresa is eccentric and a tyrant among her sisters. Or we hear that an outstanding female elementary school principal has a child who has been arrested for burglary. When frightened by women of authentic voice we even may find ourselves delighting in the wrath they evoke in those who would keep women submissive and subservient. Fear of living fully as women can lead women to collude in their own destruction and diminishment.

Facing the Invitation to Authentic Voice

The power of fear to blind our vision and shrivel our consciousness points out how important the decisions and actions are of a
woman who finds herself "standing by a river, dying of thirst." A
woman in this situation is being invited by her experience to grow
toward authentic voice and to encounter Mystery. The inner questions, the longings, the resistance and desire that are part of her
experience mark a juncture on the path to authentic voice and
authentic, mature faith. The progression is not inevitable; we are
free to refuse to grow. Still, in our depths, the desire for life is
stronger than the desire for death. Most women, however reluc-
tantly at first, make choices in the direction of richer life for themselves and their sisters.

As companions to each other, the realization of what is at stake
for us as women leads us to listen with more care to our own
voices and to the voices of others. The sounds of voices express,
even when off the mark, the desire to be a reflective self. Even the
screams of an autistic child are an effort to express a self. The
same is true for women. The crying of one abused or abandoned,
the shrewish scream of frustration, the pleading whimper, the
angry voice, the uncontrolled rage—all are efforts to express a
self, to be connected to other people, to have a dream and a vision, to voice something that can live.

The spiritual journey requires that we attend to our voices, to
their current tenor, tone and volume, and to the possibilities that
they contain. We cannot speak our wisdom if we are not reflective
about our voices. We cannot walk on the journey of faith if we do
not notice our voices and what they reveal to us about our feelings, thoughts, desires, dreams, resentments, longings, gifts, powers, and loves.

It is not easy to recognize this need to attend to our own and
to other women's voices. The patriarchal bias of the texts and
institutions of the Christian tradition have rendered women's
voices silent and women invisible. When we are accustomed to
hearing the voices of men as being worth listening to, we do not
notice the voices of women. We can, however, begin to notice
the voices of women in our Christian tradition, both our own

voices and the voices of our biblical and historical foremothers in faith.

>••<

Pause for Reflection

1. **Your Voice: A Biography.** *Take a piece of blank paper and a pencil. In the center of the paper write in capital letters, MY VOICE. Draw a circle around the phrase. Begin to think about your own voice. The questions below will help to stimulate your thinking. Use them as a springboard for your reflection, not to limit it. Jot down ideas and phrases on your paper as they come to you. Place them wherever you want on your paper.*

- *What does my voice sound like to me? When have I heard my voice played back in a recording? What was my response? Does my voice sound like that of a parent or sibling? Do I like my voice? If yes, why? If not, why not? When have I enjoyed the sound of my own voice? What happens to my voice when I laugh, scream, cry, or when I am anxious, afraid, angry, sad, peaceful, joyful?*
- *When have I been afraid to speak? When have I been told not to speak? When have I been punished for speaking?*
- *On what occasion was I pleased that I had spoken to another person or a group and pleased with what I said? When was a time that I felt bad about what I said or was frustrated that I could not express myself as I wanted to do?*
- *What people, events, dreams, desires, needs, or crises have encouraged or occasioned the development of my voice? (when I was a little girl? an adolescent? a young adult? a mature woman? a woman facing old age?) What was each of those experiences of growth in my voice like?*

When you have finished reflecting and jotting words and phrases on your piece of paper, look for the relationships among them. Look for patterns and progressions in terms of times of your life or particular questions or issues that have been companions on your journey.

Draw connecting lines among items on the page that are related. Or, group related items by enclosing them inside a line.

Once you have completed this task you can put the biography of your voice into narrative form. Possibilities include: 1) writing the biography of your voice; 2) letting your voice write its own autobiography through you; 3) writing a poem about your voice; 4) capturing the biography of your voice in music, sculpture, painting, drawing, or dance.

2. How does the idea of your voice developing through stages help you to understand your life? Identify times when you were voiceless; when you accepted unquestioningly what authorities said and repeated it; when you relied on your own inner knowledge above all else; when you enjoyed the mastery of a disciplinary or technical discourse; when you have had an authentic voice? Does the notion of forms of voice help you understand your own journey into maturity? Does it help you to understand the journey of someone else?

3. The kinds of experiences that propel women to move from one form of voice to a more developed form are those that the Christian tradition has talked about as experiences inviting encounters with Mystery. These include but are not limited to contingency, communion, moral ambiguity, collapse, disenchantment, humor, play, freedom, and courage. Thinking back over your own life, identify three experiences that may have invited you to encounter Mystery. What happened in each experience? Did you encounter Mystery? If so, what helped you to notice it? If not, what might have blocked your noticing Mystery?

4. Think about voices of women relatives, friends, coworkers, neighbors. What are their voices like? To which do you really listen? Which do you block? Pick one woman. How does her voice reflect her life as you know it to be?

5. Identify a women whom you have encountered in your life who seems to you to be a person of integrated voice. How did you respond to this woman? Were you fascinated? Did you find yourself tempted to respond in fear and envy? What happened to you because of your encounter with this woman?

6

Finding a Voice, Discovering Faith: Becoming a Public Person

ॐ

Silent No More

The Woman with the Hemorrhage

There is a scene in the story of the woman with the hemorrhage that we miss too easily: the interaction between Jesus and the woman after she has touched his clothing and he has felt healing power go out from him. We tend to move quickly over this part of the story because our attention rests on the first healing, the woman's immediate cure. But what happens in the interchange between Jesus and the woman afterward is equally important, a second healing, one contained in an invitation to find her voice and hence her faith.

As Jesus becomes conscious that healing power had gone out from him, he wheels about in the crowd and begins to ask: "Who touched my clothes?" His disciples seem almost exasperated as they respond: "You see the crowd pressing in on you; how can you say, 'Who touched me?'" (Mk 5:30–31). They miss the meaning of Jesus' question. Pressed on all sides by the crowd, Jesus is in physical contact with many. But that is not the point. Jesus intended more than physical touch when he asked his question. Power had gone out from him when he was touched by someone who recognized her deep need for healing, trusted God to meet that need, and acted on her desire for life. Whoever had touched him was at a pregnant threshold in her life. Jesus would not allow this opportunity to bring someone closer to God and herself to pass without extending the invitation to fuller life. As Mark and Luke report, despite the press of the crowd and the disciples' comment, Jesus "looked all around to see who had done it" (Mk 5:32). His was a look of compassionate love.

Now everything depends on the woman. When Jesus asks "Who touched me?" the woman realizes that her situation in relation to herself, to Jesus, and to her world has been changed. The change is more than the physically different sensations of her healed body. The change involves who she is and how she has been noticed. Her action of touching Jesus has brought her into relationship. But Jesus does not expose her against her will. He leaves her free. She must choose whether to come forward or to remain in the crowd, whether to acknowledge or reject relationship with him, whether to remain silent or to speak.[1]

The evangelists write that "the woman, knowing what had happened to her [and that her act had not gone unnoticed], came in fear and trembling, fell down before him, and told him the whole truth [related before the whole assemblage why she had touched him and how she had been instantly cured]"(Mk 5:33; Lk 8:47). A single sentence. Yet it conveys a series of transformations in the woman, transformations that highlight a crucial truth about the journey of faith: fulfillment of our desires and longings—for healing, for life, for God—comes only after we give them voice. Healing and new life come when we narrate our stories.

Consider the woman's situation. Having just touched Jesus, the Anointed One of God, and feeling God's healing power surge into her, the woman assumes she can melt back into the crowd, that her healing experience can be kept private. She thinks that she can absorb divine power and not have to relinquish anonymity, that she can experience the Kingdom and not be part of the disruption of conventional social arrangements that it inaugurates. But she is wrong. Jesus' question, "Who touched me?" startles her, focuses her awareness, and initiates a series of insights. She is no longer who she was. She is no longer invisible. Her situation in relation to herself, to Jesus, and to her world has changed irrevocably. She has touched God, and that changes everything.

No wonder the woman comes forward "trembling." She is disoriented and possibly a little afraid of the crowd. She has, after all, violated social norms by being there. More likely, though, the woman's trembling expresses her awkwardness and even fear at the new person, the healed woman she has become. She has not had time to reflect, to comprehend what she has done and what has happened to her.

The same courage that led her to touch Jesus' garment propels the woman forward now. She hears Jesus' question as a call. She responds by coming forward to acknowledge and to name what she has done and what has happened to her publicly—in the center, not at the margin. The woman gives voice to her faith by telling her story, a story that describes the act of faith: desire for God's healing that is stronger than all the rules of her social and religious world, a desire that moves her to touch Jesus, a desire that is fulfilled in instantaneous healing. The woman has moved from anonymous, invisible seeker to public evangelist.

Only then, after the woman has come forward and narrated her story, does Jesus say to her, "Daughter, your faith has made you well; go in peace, and be healed of your disease" (Mk 5:34; Lk 8:48). Only after she has narrated her encounter with the healing, liberating power of God does Jesus point out to the woman that her faith was the fulcrum of the entire event.

Until the woman gave voice to her experience, she could not know her own faith. Before she gave voice to her experience she could not have heard or understood what Jesus said to her about her faith. "Your faith has made you well," Jesus says. You are a person of power! Claim it, don't hide it. Your name is staunchly resistant, strongly desiring, powerful faith, healed one.

There is no self, no individual to be named, without voice. Jesus could not name the woman until she found her own voice. For this woman, and for contemporary Christian women, the journey to voice and the journey to faith are intimately intertwined. A woman's journey to voice is her journey in faith.

Hannah Finds Her Voice

A second story, this one from the Hebrew Scriptures, illustrates even more fully how faith grows in women as they find their voices. The story of Hannah is the story of a woman's complete movement from voicelessness to voice.

Generally interpreted as cluing us in to the fact that Samuel is special, the story of Hannah in 1 Samuel is complex and has many dimensions. I want to highlight one central dynamic: Hannah as a woman who moves from being an object to being a subject, from being mute to having a voice.[2]

In the story, Hannah, the wife of Elkanah, is infertile. This infertility occasions much pain in Hannah's life and abuse from Elkanah's second and fertile wife, Peninnah. The abuse happens particularly during the annual pilgrimage to Shiloh. As the story develops in 1 Samuel 1, while the family is at Shiloh, Hannah is weeping in response to the abuse of Peninnah. Elkanah finds her weeping and questions her: "Hannah, why do you weep and refuse to eat? Why is your heart bad? Am I not more to you than ten sons?"

In his series of questions Elkanah moves from inquiring about why she weeps (without waiting for an answer), to judging Hannah's interior disposition, to setting up a situation where she cannot speak without harming herself.[3] If Hannah answers "yes" to Elkanah's final question, "Am I not better to you than ten sons?" she denies her own experience in affirming his self-justification and his controlling interpretation of her situation. If she answers "no" to Elkanah's question, she violates social norms and could be thrown out of her known world. Instead Hannah makes a bold move easily missed because of its form: she remains silent.[4]

After the interchange Hannah rises and leaves the place where the family is eating. She walks away from husband and co-wife, who have berated and dominated her. Hannah goes to the shrine and pours her feelings forth. She desperately seeks release from the main cause of her depression by appeal to the highest authority. She cries out to God.[5]

Hannah is so immersed in expressing the pain of her unfulfilled longing that the priest at the shrine, Eli, thinks she is drunk. Like Elkanah, he questions her, "How long will you stay drunk?" Like Elkanah, Eli assumes that his observer's knowledge of Hannah is sufficient without asking her what she wants or needs or is experiencing. Like Elkanah, he assumes the role of judge and evaluates Hannah's behavior.[6] He frames his judgment in a question that calls on her to justify her behavior: "How long will you stay drunk?"

This time Hannah does not remain silent. She responds by describing her experience, her actions, and claiming her self. "I am not depressed. I am not drunk. I am pouring out my life before the Lord. I am not a worthless woman. I've been speaking out of my anxiety and grief." Hannah articulates her situation. She is considerate of her obtuse questioner but insists on articulating her feelings and needs. She names the truth about herself.[7] Eli responds by blessing Hannah. She returns to Elkanah and Peninnah, eats, and is no longer depressed. She goes back with them to Ramah.

In the final scene of the chapter Hannah discovers that she is pregnant, bears Samuel, and chooses herself when to take him to the shrine at Shiloh. When Elkanah and Hannah take the boy to Shiloh, it is on her terms. Hannah has found her voice and has become a woman of power, commitment, and capacity.[8]

Elements in Hannah's movement to voice

Hannah's story is embedded in layers of patriarchy and androcentrism. Note that the story presents Hannah as defining herself by her reproductive capacities and her ability to dedicate a son to Yahweh. This can fuel feminist criticism and even rejection of the story. But if we focus on the development of Hannah's character rather than on the cultural frame of that development, the elements in the movement to voice become clear.

Hannah has moved from voicelessness to voice. How? Her movement began in silence, a silence that bore awareness for her of the integrity and truth of her experience, a silence which sparked the perception that the way her world was arranged was not the way it had to be. She felt keenly her barrenness and her conflicted relationships with Peninnah and with her husband, but she did not run away from her feelings. Instead, by listening to herself, being receptive to her experience, Hannah developed the capacity to question her situation and to resist it. Refusing to answer her husband's questions constituted Hannah's first act of resistance; pouring out her sorrow at the shrine, her second; and responding to Eli, her third.

Hannah left her place of abuse and went to the place of holiness and hope, the shrine. At the door of the shrine she cried out to God, she mourned, and she grieved. Her public and visible expressions of her personal pain are an important part in her process of coming to voice. Public processing of pain is crucial to her transformation. When Eli accuses her of drunkenness, she speaks the truth about herself. In countering Eli, she resists the definition of herself and her reality that he would lay on her. Having been receptive to herself, having remembered that her situation could be different, she mourned her plight at the shrine and resisted both her oppression and a male-defined misunderstanding of her situation. This is the process through which Hannah develops a strong voice.

Hannah, now with voice—and voice always entails a new way of being, a new imagining of possibilities for life—returns to Ramah with Elkanah, conceives and bears Samuel, weans him, and takes him to the Lord on her own terms. She decides when to take Samuel to the shrine. Hannah has gained voice, she has gained self, she has gained power to think, to commit, and to act.

Hannah's story embodies the movement to voice The outcome is her capacity to act independently in relation to her spouse, her world, and her God. That she identifies herself and chooses to act within the constructions of her patriarchal culture does not negate the growth in voice that is hers. In her own way she stretched the limits of that patriarchal culture when she took Samuel to Shiloh on her own terms. We might wish that she had gone further and rebelled, but that is a wish that is plausible only for women who live in the late twentieth century. Whether we like the ending or not, we can learn from Hannah's story the elements of the process of coming to voice.

Voice as the Biblical Path to Faith

I have focused on the process or inner dynamics of the journey to voice in the stories of the woman with the hemorrhage and Hannah for a reason. The elements and pattern of this process are precisely those that according to the biblical tradition bring individuals and communities to faith. Conceiving the journey to voice as a journey to faith locates the experiences and struggles of contemporary Christian women within one of the biblical tradition's most fundamental processes.[9]

The first step in developing faith is an awakening or awareness that the world we occupy is not set in stone. This awareness usually arises out of an experience of pain or suffering that leads us to notice ourselves and our situation. It leads us to describe the world that we occupy and to realize that arrangements of power and resources that are accepted as givens and that clearly benefit some people and harm others are not absolute. The woman with the hemorrhage did not accept the judgment of the physicians that nothing could be done for her condition. She believed that her world could be otherwise. So too, Hannah did not accept her situation. Both women came to awareness of themselves and their worlds through experiences of pain and longing.

Her awareness of her situation leads a woman to criticize the ideology of her world: the general principles that a community uses to explain why some people have resources and others do not, why some people have power and others do not, why some people have jobs and others do not, why men are valuable and women are not. The term *ideology* is a neutral one that suggests a set of agreements by which people live together in a situation of relative safety amid limited resources and unlimited desires. A woman who can identify those agreements in her home or community or society is developing a capacity for self-transcendence, the ability to be aware of herself even as she feels, thinks, and acts in certain ways. This capacity is an essential element of psychological and spiritual maturity. It led the woman with the hemorrhage to violate the social norms of her day and seek to touch Jesus. Hannah implicitly rejected the ideology of her situation when she left the campsite and went to the shrine to mourn and grieve.

Awareness or receptivity, critique or remembering/imagining alternative worlds, and resistance, voicing that the world can be different: this cluster of attitudes, dispositions, imaginings, and actions is crucial to developing faith.[10] Notice that any separate element of this cluster or all of them together lead an individual to a deeper sense of independent self. Any one or all lead an individual toward identifying and thereby separating from religious traditions and political and social power structures, so that she can develop a critical relationship to them. Any one or all of this cluster of attitudes, dispositions, imaginings, and actions move a woman toward trusting and acting on her own authority. This is what Hannah did when she moved from her silent awareness and refusal to her firm response to the priest Eli. She voiced her resistance to Eli's interpretation of her situation and instead narrated her own experience. This is what the woman with the hemorrhage did when she touched Jesus's garment and again when she came forward and narrated her encounter with divine power.

The biblical journey to faith is neither cerebral nor solitary. Once a woman acknowledges her pain and becomes aware of the ideologies supporting the androcentrism and patriarchy that diminish and limit her, she must do something with the pain that she is experiencing. If she represses it or denies it, she cannot move. She must express her pain through an act or acts that are public and social in order for it to be transformed. She must embody her pain in an external way in order for her to continue to move on the journey of faith. Hannah's weeping and expressing her sorrow at the shrine provide one example.

In their stories the woman with the hemorrhage and Hannah reenact the movement to faith and freedom contained in the Exodus story, the archetypal story of God for the Jewish people. In Exodus, the Hebrew people were enslaved in Egypt. At some point they became aware of themselves in their slavery and realized that this was not how the world had to be. The Hebrew people rejected the ideology of imperial Egypt when they cried out to God in their pain. They confronted Pharaoh with God's command to let them leave Egypt. They gained the capacity to demand their freedom, however, only after they had publicly "cried out" in their pain. The world-changing response to their cries, according to Exodus, was that "God heard their cry."[11]

Crying out in pain is a dangerous and powerfully subversive act, made more so when done corporately. Power structures—whether those of ancient Egypt, where the Hebrew people were enslaved; those of Hannah's time; those of Palestine during Roman occupation; or those of our own country today—deny the existence of pain and suffering in the lives of people. When they cannot pretend that pain does not exist, they minimize and delegitimize it by encouraging individuals to endure pain privately and to take total responsibility for any pain in their lives.

Oppressive cultural and institutional forces work insidiously to keep those who suffer both silent and isolated. A friend who led an ecumenical retreat for women related to me that many women at the retreat told her they had been taught that friendships among women are temptations to the sin of lesbianism and therefore to be avoided at all costs. Before Vatican II many women religious in the Roman Catholic Church received such admonitions as well. And even when the teaching to avoid strong bonds with other women is not presented explicitly and forcefully by religious institutions, many women pick up the message from husbands, fathers, and brothers, who fear losing women's attentions. Such formal and informal messages work effectively to keep women isolated from each other and subservient to men.

More broadly in our society, the decided preference for individual, psychological interpretations of problems rather than sociological or political explanations suggests the success of power structures at isolating individuals in their oppressive situations. Psychological pain provides the illusion that an individual is responsible and therefore capable of solving all problems. Sociological and political explanations of problematic situations reveal to individuals just how enmeshed they are in structures and communities larger than individuals alone. This insight generates a sense of vulnerability and fear, both of which dominant cultural forces in the United States deny and despise. Hence the culture itself teaches values that shore up current political and social arrangements and help to silence the voices of those who are harmed by them.

When a woman is willing to express her personal pain in community with other women also willing to express their pain, it generates a communal anger that may develop into risky but real social power. When individuals risk feeling and expressing their pain with others, the cry of pain begins the formation of a new community around an alternative perception of reality. The source of such a counter-community is trust in one's pain and in the pain of one's neighbor, which is very much like one's own.[12]

When the woman with the hemorrhage narrated what had happened to her, she was inviting the people in the crowd, who had hemmed Jesus in by pressing so on all sides, to admit that they touched Jesus too, that they also were in need of healing. The gospel story does not tell us how the crowd responded. What is important for us, however, is that the woman implicitly called forth a community formed around an alternative perception of reality, one that says God's power is available to those who desire it, even the unclean. When Hannah mourned and cried at the entrance of the shrine she modeled a new/old way of relating to God—new because she brought her personal pain to the shrine, old because she publicly expressed that pain.[13] This, joined with the way she responded to Eli by describing her situation—"I am not drunk, I am a sorrowing woman"—called forth a community formed around the strength that comes from telling the truth of a woman's experience. Hannah imagined and enacted a new way of being in the world as a woman and by so doing invites all the women who come after her to join her. So too were the Hebrew people creating something new when they confronted Pharaoh repeatedly with Yahweh's demand that he let the people leave Egypt. They were calling forth a community that would not accept political power arrangements as the ultimate authority and arbiter of peoples' lives.

Fear of the social power of alternative communities formed out of shared pain explains why groups of women or persons of color or other marginalized people are considered dangerous by society. Martin Luther King, Jr., was labeled a Communist when he pointed out that disproportionate numbers of poor and black men were being sent to Vietnam to fight. Women who speak out in the church are labeled radical feminists by the Vatican Congregation for the Doctrine of the Faith. Some Christian feminists are called daughters of Satan. Labeling oppressed persons who voice their pain and identify structural problems as people who are politically unacceptable, psychologically disturbed, or in other ways dangerous is another technique for containing the subversive power of pain.[14]

The public processing of pain is crucial for transformation of individuals and communities. It is the pathway out of "the system" and into the embrace of God, present in the promise of an imagined better future. Biblical theologian Walter Brueggemann considers the pivotal power of pain to be the Bible's most dangerous insight and the one that may contribute most to us.[15] If this is true, then the pain that women feel in the church and in society today is a powerful force that can lead to new life, if it is expressed. If it is not, it will lead only to diminishment and death. We must move. We cannot remain forever "standing by the river, dying of thirst."

The public processing of pain permits and evokes the imagining and redescription of reality that creates a space for newness. In the story of Hannah, her pouring out of her heart to God at the entrance to the shrine at Shiloh led her to speak clearly to Eli, to begin to act differently in the world. She ceased to act like a barren and discarded woman. Instead, she acted like a woman of worth and stature. The story of the woman with the hemorrhage does not describe her grief or tears, but one can imagine them a part of her days and nights as she went from doctor to doctor for years and then turned to God's power as her only resource. The Israelites' cry of pain, which probably took place in liturgical settings, evoked so powerfully in them the memory of being a people—the descendants of Abraham, Isaac, and Jacob—that it made risky political action possible.

From pain-inspired imaginings that envision an alternative reality come the release of new social possibilities. This dynamic rests at the heart of the foundational story of the Jewish people, the Exodus story. The Israelites became Yahweh's chosen people in a new way—liturgically, politically, and legislatively—the moment God led them out of Egypt.[16] The woman with the hemorrhage was cured immediately, healed by her faith, a faith that imagined another way for her to be in the world. And Hannah lived the possibility of being a fruitful woman.

The release of shared visions or new imagination does not always have an immediate external social component, but it always has at least an implicit one. In the Exodus story the social dimension is explicit. It is a people, a community, that is formed by God through the Exodus experience. In the story of Hannah we have in its earliest form the fruits of imagination that will change all of history. Hannah's son, Samuel, will play a crucial role as prophet for God's people. So Hannah's capacity to imagine a different life for herself, and then to live that life when the possibility becomes reality—she returns to Ramah, bears Samuel, and takes him to Shiloh on her own terms—influences all that the Jewish and Christian peoples will call salvation history.

Within the context of canonical texts, the stories of Exodus, Hannah, and the woman with the hemorrhage have positive outcomes. This can lead us away from noticing just how disruptive the actions of these people were, how risky they were. Living faithfully is no guarantee of a smooth or happy ending, especially when the actions one takes—claiming one's integrity as a woman in church or in society, becoming politically active to protect women and children, or any other—raise up the blindness and even positive harmfulness of one's church, neighborhood, city, family, or religious community. An act of faithfulness—whether love, fidelity, prophetic proclamation, or daily nurturing—can cost everything. But there is no other way to move.

The journey to voice is the journey to faith

The elements and pattern of the journey to voice are the very same characteristics that the biblical tradition identifies in stories of individuals and communities who come to authentic faith. Connecting our experiences as contemporary women of faith to the Christian heritage through a biblically identified process of growth and development—rather than through a particular doctrine or principle—expands the range of ideas, actions, and feelings available to us in our efforts to be faithful. It relates women to the tradition more holistically, through ourselves and our stories, rather than through obligation to an external authority or ideal. This intimate connection creates space for contemporary women to imagine ourselves and our relationships to God and to our religious heritages in more ways. Connected to our religious heritage through a process of journeying to faith that transcends any particular theological articulation, historical time period, or set of institutional leaders, we are freer to embrace ourselves and to grow in faith.

Truncated Journeys and Silenced Voices

Seeing ourselves on the journey to voice-faith-wisdom offers possibilities for women. It offers, perhaps, a path through which some can remain connected to their religious heritage with integrity and with the experiential knowledge that it can be life-giving for them. At the same time, conceiving their situation in terms of the journey to voice invites women to develop a realistic perspective on the situation of their foremothers in faith and themselves. For while the stories of Hannah and the woman with the hemorrhage reveal to us the process of women who do come to voice, not all scriptural stories turn out so well for women. While Hannah, the women with the hemorrhage, and others are able to negotiate the journey to voice and faith successfully, this is not true for all women in scripture. Some women never have the chance to begin the journey to voice and faith. Others are prevented from completing the journey. Sometimes their circumstances leave them little room for freedom of action. At other times their stories are truncated or hidden because they do not serve the purpose of the writer. Three examples illustrate the reality of truncated journeys and silenced voices.

Jephthah's daughter complies with a foolish vow of her father. In thanksgiving for victory in battle, her father promises to sacrifice to Yahweh the first person who comes out of his dwelling upon his return. Jephthah's daughter comes out to greet her father and thereby becomes the sacrificial victim. She manages minimally to shape her conditions for dying when she requests two months in which to mourn her virginity before she is sacrificed (Jgs 11). Even though her voice is silenced by her father's need to keep his vow to God, the women of Israel remember her, and in their remembrance give her voice again. But she does not have a full voice. She has no time to become a woman, to have an identity and a name other than Jephthah's daughter.

The concubine who is so raped and abused that she dies and then is dismembered by her master—who sends her body parts to the tribes of Israel—has neither name nor voice (Jgs 19).[17] She is thrown out to the men of the town to assuage their evil desires, and her body is then used to broadcast the message of their evil to all the tribes of Israel. She is consumed by the evil of others—so totally consumed that the scriptures attribute to her no voice, no sound, not even a groan of pain.[18]

Jephthah's daughter and the concubine are cut off. Voiceless and nameless, their stories have nothing to do with their own journeys to faith. They are used by men. Their stories make it clear that patriarchal societies deny some women not only the journey to voice and to faith but life itself. As the extreme cases, they emphasize how much patriarchal societies and religions obstruct that journey for all women.

The story of Miriam, sister of Moses and mother of the Hebrew people, reveals an alternative but equally problematic reality for women who undertake the journey to voice in a patriarchal society. The forces of that society will constrain women who do find their voices.

In the climactic scene of delivery from Egypt in Exodus, Miriam dances and sings her praise for Yahweh's power when the Egyptians are drowned in the Reed Sea. Her song is echoed in the Magnificat of Mary, the Mother of Jesus. Later in the story of the

Israelites in the desert, however, the writer has God punish Miriam for questioning Moses. She is punished because her voice is too strong.[19]

The biblical heritage, then, contains the same ambiguity with reference to women's journeys to voice as does the situation of women's lives today. The text contains stories of women who find and use their voices, of women who are cut down before they find their voices, and of women punished for their voices. The biblical texts are as patriarchal and androcentric as was the world from which they come. Hence, the stories of women in these texts convey the difficulties of the journey to voice and faith for women: the difficulty of surviving the journey to voice and the potentially dangerous consequences awaiting women who do develop their voices. At the same time, the biblical texts offer more than patriarchy and androcentrism to women.

Pause for Reflection

1. Review this definition of androcentric thinking from chapter 2:

An androcentric world is male-centered. It assumes: 1) that male and human are the same thing; 2) that because they are identical "the generic masculine habit of thought, language, and research is adequate" to understanding human beings; and, 3) that "when women, per se, are considered, . . . they are discussed as an object, exterior to mankind, needing to be explained and fitted into one"s world view," like "trees" or "unicorns." In an androcentric world, then, women are basically marginal [quotations from Gross, "Androcentrism and Androgyny," in *Beyond Androcentrism*]. What matters in an androcentric world is what men want, do, and value. Women's activities and values are not considered important. They are secondary at best.

Identify a time when you encountered androcentric thinking. Identify a time when you yourself used androcentric thinking. What happened to your sense of yourself in each situation?

2. The woman with the hemorrhage thought she could remain invisible after she had received God's healing power through touching Jesus. Instead, she discovers that she is bidden to proclaim what God has done for her in her life. When have you tried to remain invisible to yourself or to others? When have you been called to proclaim what God has done in your life?

3. Read the story of Hannah in I Samuel 1 and review the description of Hannah's journey to voice in the chapter. Write a letter to Hannah in which you tell her about your own struggles, grief, and sorrow as a woman in the church and in society. When you have finished the letter read it aloud to Hannah. What does Hannah say to you in response? What will you remember of what she says?

4. This chapter claims that the journey to voice is a journey to faith for women. How does this understanding change your view of what growing in faith means for you?

7

Voice as Faith: Women's Path

৯৵৲৯

Feminist Spirituality, Voice, and Faith

If the process of the journey to voice shares a fundamental orientation and crucial elements with the process of the journey to faith exemplified in the Exodus story, Hannah, and the woman with the hemorrhage, the same process is described also by women who write and work in women's spirituality. What makes these women's writings valuable to women is precisely that they offer guidance to women about how to move along the journey to voice, to faith, to wisdom.

Maria Harris in *Dance of the Spirit* discusses women's spirituality as a spiraling dance that moves through moments like those we have seen in the journey to voice and the journey to faith. Her presentation accents the ways that women's spiritual growth involves developing voices and selves in community.[1]

Harris describes the process of women's spiritual development not as progression through a series of stages or as steps on a stair or a ladder but as steps in a dance, steps that turn back on each other and weave together. The movement of these steps propels women toward self and voice. Harris's steps include receptivity, remembering, resistance, ritual mourning, and rebirth or artistry.

Harris's movement begins with *receptivity*, a particular kind of silent awareness. This is not the silence of voicelessness but the silence that is the human capacity to listen to Being. It is the capacity to listen to our longing, the ability to notice accurately whatever reality is around us and to begin to locate ourselves in relation to it. It is the capacity and courage to notice and attend to all of our feelings as we face our situations individually and corporately as women in a profoundly patriarchal world. In this place of silence or receptivity we discover that we are subjects of history, that we can act, create, change things. This receptivity or silence is, in reality, a waking up to ourselves and our life.[2]

This receptivity or silence is the beginning place of awareness of self and other. It is the beginning of unlearning not to speak. It is the beginning of deep quiet, which allows the center or integral self to emerge. This makes possible experiencing self—becoming a self—in relation to others and the Ultimate Other, God.

The space of receptivity or silence, if a woman does not flee from it, evokes *remembering*. Remembering has two dimensions. The first is a hermeneutic of suspicion—remembering that things could be otherwise, have been otherwise, and that the way things are supports power for some and oppression for others. This is remembering that the way the world is arranged is not cast in stone or preordained by God.[3] This dimension of remembering is crucial to renegotiating our relationship to the Christian heritage because it opens up possibilities for newness. It invites us to imagine and desire a different future for ourselves, our sisters, and our daughters in the church.

The second dimension of remembering, empowered by the first, is the remembering of suffering. The stories of tragedy and travesty must be remembered, says Harris. Among those stories Harris mentions are the burning of more than a million European witches, a story largely untold in the history of Christianity; the genital mutilation of millions of African women by the quiet compliance of too many missionaries; the death by burning of millions of Indian women; the destruction of the feet of millions of our Chinese foremothers, crippling them for life; and the still continuing practice of womb and breast mutilation in so-called "advanced" nations such as our own where unnecessary mastectomies and hysterectomies have never been protested.[4]

Remembering pain and suffering is not easy, but unless we are willing to remember and to give voice to these experiences they will be repeated. Silence allows oppression to continue. The need to make sure that these experiences are not forgotten and not ignored, the need to tell the stories of those who have suffered, moves women to voice.[5]

The remembering Harris describes is vital to women's finding their voices. It also constitutes a major challenge to women's growth. The temptation is to avoid the memories of suffering in order to avoid the unpleasantness, the grief, the anger, and the rage that women feel when they face the history and the present reality of women's oppression and abuse in the church and in society. Facing this reality can lead women destructively in three directions: fear, self-loathing, and consuming rage.

Fear leads women to live their lives on the margins, to conform to dominant social mores in their class and culture in order to avoid abuse. Women driven by this fear try desperately to be good so that no harm will come to them. Guilt overwhelms them when they are harmed because they perceive their lives as a direct consequence of their own ability to achieve perfection, a state defined for them by others.

Self-loathing is self-hatred, a desire for self-destruction. It is rooted in a disoriented desire, sometimes spoken and sometimes not, that one not be a woman, and the desire that one's daughters not have been born female. Such hatred destroys, sapping energy, creativity, will, and desire. It leads to addictions of various kinds.

The third potentially destructive consequence of remembering is consuming rage, the blind rage that traps a woman in a cycle of hatred of others as well as self. This is the undifferentiated anger that never stops, that feeds upon itself and engenders the desire to destroy.

These three destructive consequences of remembering are not the end of the story. Women have other options, but for these other options to become real, women must be willing to enter fully into their experience of remembering, to notice, name, and accept the feelings that come when they remember, without labeling them good or bad. Remembering is a crucible in women's lives, an experience that can purify and strengthen as well as destroy. Because it is so potent, remembering is best done in community, not alone.

When remembering leads to life, it strengthens women, focuses their energy and attention, and leaves them with a stronger sense of self. With a more developed sense of themselves in the world, women are able to move on to another step in Harris's dance of the spirit: resistance.

Resistance is constituted by an attitude of questioning, an un-willingness to believe easily what we are told about self, others, world, God. To resist means making questioning part of our spiritual discipline. It also means refusing to set closure, to say that all the information is in—perhaps especially about the revelation of God.[6] When we resist, we choose the living, pulsating faith of a living relationship with God over the intellectual or emotional satisfaction and safety of an incomplete understanding of God and of ourselves.

Resistance involves being willing to question the truthfulness of what authorities say. It means understanding that all ideas, stories, and practices privilege some people and take privilege from others. Women who resist are willing to consider that when authorities in the church speak, they do so with good intentions that can have unintended negative consequences, consequences of which the authorities are quite unaware. Resisting women understand that reality is more complex than those with power comprehend. Women who resist are willing to make judgments about what the authorities say and do. They are willing to deem actions and statements unfaithful when they violate women's best inner discernment about faith based on their experiences of God and their understanding of scripture and theology. Women who resist are already being fed by what is life-giving in the Christian heritage, especially its promise that God longs for all to have full, rich lives.

The movement from resistance in Harris's scheme is to *ritual mourning*. Mourning and grieving have to take place before we can move on to new acts. Mourning puts an ending to things lost or given up. It cleanses and opens us to what will come. Women must mourn their abuse; their rape; their unwantedness; their losses; the voices, projects, life, and dignity that have been denied or stolen from them.[7]

Mourning is a passageway between remembering and rebirth or artistry, the act of creating something new. It is not an easy space to occupy. Grieving or mourning often involves bodily distress and an intense preoccupation with the image of who/what was lost. It involves guilt and a disconcerting lack of warmth. One who grieves finds her life disorganized, without meaningful pattern.[8] One who grieves often feels like a misfit, aware of a chasm in the world that no one else sees.

These characteristics of bereaved persons are common in women beginning to face their pasts. Persons who mourn move through the stages of grief outlined by Elisabeth Kübler-Ross: denial, anger, bargaining, depression, and acceptance. Anger is an especially real part of mourning for many women. It is not a deadly sin or a human failure. Rather, as ethicist Beverly Harrison has written:

> Anger is better understood as a feeling-signal that all is not well in our relation to other persons or groups or the world around us. Anger is a mode of connectedness to others and it is always a vivid form of caring. To put the point another way: anger is—and it ALWAYS is—a sign of some resistance in ourselves to the moral quality of the social relations in which we are immersed. Extreme and intense anger signals a deep reaction to the action upon us or toward others to whom we are related.[9]

The anger in our mourning signals deep concern for the relationships in our lives. This helps to explain why mourning cannot remain private. Mourning that ends at the personal stage clogs and clots our coming to voice; it chokes. Mourning must become communal. It becomes so when we share our own losses and sufferings with others and come to identify with the losses and sufferings of our companions. This is why Harris calls for ritual mourning. It is a central focus of the plethora of women's rituals being created and practiced today both inside and outside denominational structures.

Women who are "standing by the river, dying of thirst" have much to mourn. They mourn all that the Christian tradition has failed to give them. They mourn their unfulfilled longings. They mourn their status as second-class and invisible beings in the church and in society. They mourn the loss of their unconsciousness, the time before they saw the dimensions of their situation and began to feel the pain.

Sometimes it feels as though the mourning and grief will never end, that one's tears and anger are all that constitute existence, that one's broken-heartedness will color every moment and perception of the future. In these times personal courage, the support of women who understand, and deliberate ritualizing of the experience can help a woman move through the process of mourning. Mourning is a process that has its own time.

Out of ritual mourning comes *artistry* or *rebirth:* the embodiment, revelation, and release of something new.[10] Out of this holistic response to ourselves and our lives, creative voice emerges. Women, in the image of God, create through the spoken and embodied word.

For women who are experiencing frustrated longing and dislocation in relation to their religious heritage, the fruits of artistry or rebirth are varied. Some women become activists, some express newfound freedom and joy in art or in service. Some women make major changes in their lives because they cannot go back to who or what they were before. Some women reject the institutional church or limit their contact with it. Other women seek out or develop settings for prayer and spiritual growth that are nurturing for them. Still others commit to companioning their sisters on the journey to God. Whatever the outcome, artistry or rebirth leads women to claim zones of freedom and life in a church and a society that are at best neutral and more often hostile to women acting freely.

Receptivity, remembering, resisting, ritual mourning, and rebirth are key moments in the spiritual journey through which women come to themselves, come to have powerful voices. They are the embodied, cognitive, affective, and social dynamics through which women grow in faith.

Voice as Faith: A Place to Stand

The process of the journey to voice and faith is variously described by feminist theorists, by biblical theologians, and by writers on women's spirituality. From their different perspectives and distinctive purposes, all focus on a process of interior transformation that radically changes a woman's sense of self and so alters her relationship to herself, her world, and her religious heritage.

Journey to voice and faith is an image or metaphor. As with any compelling image, this image offers women an altered space within which to experience themselves and their worlds. The image of journey to voice and faith focuses women's attention toward their own processes of growth and life, toward the inner human dynamics that incarnate whatever truths religious traditions seek to convey. Journey as process is not tied to a particular principle, theology, role, person, community, historical period, hierarchy, or institutional structure. The image of journey to voice and faith recasts truth for the spiritual life from something external and imposed to something disclosed to mind and heart as a woman embraces her unique life.

Offering another place from which to relate to and assess our religious tradition, the image of journey to voice and faith creates space within which we can work with materials from the tradition that are androcentric and patriarchal yet still find them revelatory. Focusing on the process of the journey to voice allows us to discern and claim the deeper movements of God in these androcentric scriptures, movements that may, when ritually embodied, speak to women across the barrier of their androcentrism. Hence, we may be able to employ even androcentric texts as resources on our journeys to God.

The journey to voice and faith provides a place of shared experiences that may connect contemporary women to our biblical and historical foremothers in faith. Consciously identifying the similarities and differences between our foremothers' and our own journeys further turns the Christian heritage into a resource. This identification reveals the life-giving and death-dealing dimensions of our foremothers' relationships to their religious tradition. Having seen both in their stories, we find ourselves bidden to face the life-giving and death-dealing elements of our own church and world. And, having seen these elements, we are thrust back to our own lives as the place where we do and will encounter God. We are weaned away from the expectation that someone or something other—authority figure, institution, religious congregation—will care for us, guide us, take us to God. The journey is our own, in conversation with, and sometimes outside of conversation with, our religious heritage and our companions in community. When we relate to our religious tradition in this way, we are following a path toward wisdom used by our foremothers in faith—a path of faithful, critical, expectant discrimination of what is for life and what is not in our Christian heritage.

The journey to voice allows us to see that spiritual and psychological processes essential to women's full development are deeply rooted in the biblical heritage. A woman is called to a life of faithfulness and response to God's call, not an existence of static, mindless acquiescence to existence and submission to her situation. Faith requires nothing less than a woman's responding "yes" to an invitation to full personhood, to whatever particular shape personhood takes for each one.

If we are willing to trust that a process presented in both biblical and feminist resources is essential to our psychological and spiritual development as human beings and persons of faith, we will find ourselves with a rich mixture of resources against which to discern, interpret, and act on our own journeys. The journey to voice expands the range of ways that a woman can relate to her religious tradition. The processes of growth and change involved in this journey are negotiated sometimes within and sometimes over against authoritative teachings, institutional structures, and cultural conventions. Because the journey is a process, a woman who walks it finds herself in differing relationship to her religious heritage at different moments in the journey. A woman relating to her religious heritage in this way may find herself freed from orienting herself to it primarily through compliance or opposition. At the same time, she may find herself called to claim and take responsibility for her own relationship with God, herself, and her world in ways that she never has before.

The journey to voice and faith is a metaphor of shared experiences for contemporary Christian women and their foremothers. It provides a space within which to think about and discern the movements of our journeys to God, a space within which we can be keenly aware of but finally not defined by the androcentrism and patriarchy of our contexts. It offers a place from which contemporary women of faith can criticize our religious tradition, our society, and our own lives. It offers the ground, the place on which to stand, so that we can criticize Christianity's androcentrism from within the tradition itself. It also is the place from which we as women can elaborate and theologize out of our own experiences of God and of life.

The biblical description of the journey to faith and feminist psychology's and spirituality's description of the movement to voice converge. This provides contemporary women of faith multiple communities of wisdom and discourse against which to test our experiences and ideas as we negotiate the journey to voice. Multiple warranting and testing of experiences and ideas provides a more trustworthy context within which to live. Using both Wisdom traditions supports contemporary women of faith as we return to the originating stories of the tradition in scripture and history that involve women and as we look expectantly for a path that can be life-giving rather than death-dealing in relation to our heritage. Our new relationship with ourselves and our religious heritage can provide a stronger and more independent warrant for our own identity as Christian women and generate greater freedom of action in relating to our churches.

The journey to voice and faith, then, is a metaphoric space, a place for women of faith to stand, a zone of freedom within which to breathe, think, feel, and grow. That place can become the foundation for critique of self, world, and church, and a fountain of images and inspiration to fund our imaginations as we deal with unprecedented challenges.

Journey to Faith and Voice in a Patriarchal Theological Tradition

When women come to understand that their journey to voice is their journey to faith, they turn a more critical attention to the way their religious heritage has been elaborated in theology and practice. They become attuned to the explicit and implicit theological interpretations of Christianity that reinforce patriarchy and justify the abuse and oppression of women. So, for example, women notice and reject interpretations of The Fall story in Genesis that make women responsible for evil and suffering in the world. Or they resist pointedly the efforts of the National Conference of Catholic Bishops to create a pastoral letter on women that does not reflect their voices. Or women clergy notice that when they gather together at clergy conferences, male clergy often want to know who gathered and why and begin to attack the group for being separatist. Carrying out the critique of teachings and practices in the tradition that are detrimental to women is an integral dimension of women's journeys to faith and voice. While all the classical theological themes are in need of critique, a theme of particular importance to women who locate themselves on the journey to voice and faith is that of the human person.

The tradition's theological anthropology—view of the human person—was one of the first themes criticized by early contemporary feminist theologians. Their constructive work in this area has continued unabated for over twenty-five years.[11] An early and continuing feminist critique has been directed toward the doctrine of sin as it has been presented by male theologians in their writings on the human person. This critique serves to illustrate the importance of the constructive work of feminist theologians today to women of faith and to the integrity of the Christian theological tradition.

Most Christian theology has been written by men and in the light of their experiences. This theology has rested on the assumption that when men have described their experiences and ideas, then the "human" experience, including that of women, has been adequately described and explained. But as feminist theologians point out, this is a profoundly androcentric view. Feminist theologians criticize androcentric theology and history for presenting an incomplete picture of human beings and of the Christian community's life, one that has omitted the particular experiences, social contexts, and challenges of women. As a result, the tradition's theology of sin as popularly taught has serious negative consequences for women's journeys to faith.

The most widely shared Christian understanding of sin defines it as prideful self-assertion. This self-assertion is the result of man (as invariably stated) trying to make himself the whole or center of existence, when he knows he is only a part, a creature. Humans act in this way, say the theologians, because they suffer from anxiety, an anxiety that results from knowing that they are free and at the same time, finite or limited.[12] This definition of the root of sin assumes that the human person has a strong sense of self, in fact an excessively strong sense of self. While that assumption might be true for some or even the majority of men throughout history, feminist psychology suggests that it is decidedly inaccurate for the majority of women for the past two centuries at least and certainly in the last half of the twentieth century. Women struggle to develop a sense of self with clear boundaries. The struggle is a constitutive element of their journey to voice.

Working from a male-defined view of sin, Christian theologians define grace as leading to self-giving, self-sacrificial love, the capacity to extend oneself for the welfare of others, even at a cost to the individual.[13] Self-giving and self-sacrifice are important components of love to be learned and practiced by persons with strongly developed senses of self.

There is no question that the love of mature persons involves the capacity to extend themselves for others. The problem comes when self-sacrificing love is preached to persons with little or no sense of self. Such teaching is profoundly damaging to them psychologically and spiritually. Women largely are identified and defined by their caregiving relationships to others. Many women experience a sense of self and worth only as reflected in the opinion others hold of them. Further, many women are incapable of identifying their own desires. Consequently, to think about women's sinfulness and growth in faith in terms developed from the experience of men is more than inappropriate, it is sinful. Only after the Christian tradition has built up a long and vigorous practice of helping women to become strong, centered selves, of helping women find their voices, will its teachings about sinful pride be existentially intelligible to women.[14]

If those charged with the pastoral care of women want to help them grow in faith, they need to attend to the dynamics of women's experiences. Women, socialized to be part of a larger whole and to view the world through the eyes of others, have a different set of temptations to sin than men. As feminist theologian Valerie Saiving puts it:

> The specifically feminine forms of sin—"feminine" not because they are confined to women or because women are incapable of sinning in other ways but because they are outgrowths of the basic feminine character structure—have a quality which can never be encompassed by such terms as "pride" and "will-to-power." They are better suggested by such items as triviality, distractibility, and diffuseness; lack of an organizing center or focus; dependence on others for one's own self-definition; tolerance at the expense of standards of excellence; inability to respect the boundaries of privacy; sentimentality, gossipy sociability, and mistrust of reason—in short, underdevelopment or negation of the self.[15]

Saiving's list of women's temptations constitutes a cluster of behaviors and impulses that lead women away from finding their voices and developing centered, integrated selves. Her list suggests an exaggerated and unhealthy concern for other persons, a lack of self-definition if not a positive fear of being an independent self, an inability to focus on creative projects or passions in a sustained manner, the inability to recognize or act on their own longings. Saiving's list suggests a sustained flurry of activity and emotional attachments through which a woman can avoid facing her own heart's desire as well as the pain and oppressive power relationships that define her situation. These behaviors describe women who have not found their own voices.

If Saiving's list of women's temptations is true and accurate for large numbers of women (if not for all), then the Christian tradition's most widely held definition of sin—pride—and its solution—self-sacrificing love—are profoundly unhelpful for women. In fact, they keep women in their sin of self-negation. They keep them giving out of a drained emptiness instead of out of an abundant fullness of self, gifts, and awareness of God's love. Healthy self-sacrifice is possible only for persons who have a self. For them, it is transformed into willingly expended attention and energy that are not experienced as sacrifice but as loving action, gladly undertaken. Failing to make these crucial discriminations, popular Christian teaching drives women further into guilt and self-abuse.

The lack of a focused self or of authentic voice is a crucial problem for women. The issues that revolve around it—Saiving's list of attitudes, tendencies, and behaviors—are the temptations that women face on their journeys to voice. Because the Christian theological tradition has not adequately explored the distinctive experiences of women, what theologians, pastors, and even other women say to women about sin, salvation, and God's love actually may harm them and constitute an obstacle on their journeys to God. Reconceiving women's journeys in faith as the development of voice provides an alternative ground from which to approach and interpret the Christian heritage.[16]

Given the overwhelmingly androcentric and patriarchal bias of the Christian tradition, how can women receive help instead of harm from it on their journeys to God? The answer, I believe, is to encounter the tradition on the journey to voice, knowing that it is both resource and obstacle, and to trust that as one's voice develops, one is being led toward wise faith. Such an encounter involves a persistent dialogue between what the community of women say about their own experiences of growth in voice and faith and the stories and theologies that are part of the Christian heritage. The outcomes of the dialogue must be tested constantly in terms of their fruits. Does the theology or action that results move a woman in the direction of fuller rather than diminished life? Does the theology that results fund creative imagining about the future for a woman, her immediate community, and the world? Does the action that results lead to greater and truer harmony for a woman and for those with whom she is in relationship? Rich, full life is the fruit of Wisdom in the biblical tradition. Wise faith perceives, articulates, and supports people and actions that enrich life in this way. But wise faith knows that the actions toward richer, fuller, life are not without pain and conflict, especially when the steps one chooses disrupt the status quo.

Coming to Faithful Voice

The journey to voice and the journey to faith are not separate journeys for women. They are integrally and intimately connected, so much so that for us the journey to voice *is* a journey to faith. Women cannot experience the depths and plumb the richness of faith, cannot know our own faith fully until we find our voices. Without developing her voice, a woman does not come to mature, effective faith. Without growth in voice a woman cannot speak her experience, her wisdom, her knowledge of God. When a woman finds herself bidden to speak about her own experience, she also is bidden to speak about God's presence and action in her life. She is called to faithful voice. Women who find themselves "standing by the river, dying of thirst" are being invited to walk the journey to faithful voice. Undertaking that journey recasts a woman's relationship to herself, her religious heritage, and her church.

Pause for Reflection

1. Maria Harris talks about the process of women's spiritual development as a spiraling dance from receptivity through remembering, resistance, and ritual mourning to rebirth. Identify times in your own life when you moved through this process. Which parts of it do you enter easily? Which do you resist? Why?

2. Journey to voice and faith is an image or metaphor. It offers an imaginative space within which to perceive, feel, and think about yourself and your Christian tradition. How does imagining yourself on a journey to voice and faith shift the way you think and feel about yourself? Your capacities? Your religious tradition? Explain.

3. Valerie Saiving's list of temptations common to women include "such items as triviality, distractibility, and diffuseness; lack of an organizing center or focus; dependence on others for one's own self-definition; tolerance at the expense of standards of excellence; inability to respect the boundaries of privacy; sentimentality, gossipy sociability, and mistrust of reason—in short, underdevelopment or negation of the self" (Saiving, "The Human Situation," 108–9). Think about the items in her list. Which have been part of your life? What has it cost you to give in to your particular temptations? When and how did you resist one of them in some situation in your life?

8

Walking Wisdom's Path

কুৎৎ

A Question Revisited

We began with a question. What does a woman do when she awakens to the intensity of her longing for God and faces her pain, realizing that her religious heritage has frustrated her longing, that it has been death-dealing for her? Can this moment of difficult realization be a gift to her in any way? To put it slightly differently, Is hope that creative possibility may emerge anything more than self-delusion when a woman finds herself "standing by a river, dying of thirst"?

The question captures the existential situation of many Christian women today. It is a complex question, one that involves a woman's psychological and spiritual development, her social, cultural, and economic contexts, her relationship to her religious heritage, to the community that carries that heritage, and her relationship to God. How she handles the question has consequences for all dimensions of her life.

There is no way a woman can answer the question from a distanced, objective standpoint. She cannot get outside of herself to weigh the facts of the situation dispassionately. Her response to the experience of frustrated longing and disappointment is a matter of integrity and an act of faith. She is bidden to answer the question while in the midst of a significant moment in her spiritual development: an experience of disillusionment.

Disillusionment and Wisdom

We are not accustomed to thinking of experiences of disillusionment as potentially positive, as opportunities for growth. The dominant religious and secular cultures of the contemporary United States respond to disillusionment harshly. A cynicism that derides the foolishness of those who dare to hope is one common response. Another is emotional distress that spirals into numbing depression. Obsessive controlling behavior, mindless conformity to an external authority, addictions of various kinds, blind rage, violence, a consuming acquisitiveness, self-loathing, shame, unbridled self-absorption, apathy, and an emotional chaos through which one abdicates responsibility for self—all are destructive ways that individuals seek to avoid experiences of disillusionment. Each strategy brings its own particular form of diminishment or death. Yet women are tempted to any one or more of these by a culture that says anyone who is disillusioned has been a fool.

Our situation as the twentieth century comes to an end shows how far our churches and our secular culture have moved away from basic insight into the dynamics of the human spirit. Negotiating experiences of disillusionment, with all the pain and loss that that involves, is necessary for a human being to mature and to gain insight. Healthy adulthood is not achieved until we have negotiated experiences of disillusionment and done so in a way that leaves us deeper, stronger, and wiser. Denying that disillusionment can bring insight and lacking rituals that structure the experience for us, we have become a culture where adolescence continues ever further into an individual's chronological span and where mature adulthood is rarely reached. Traditional cultures knew that negotiating disillusionment was essential to maturing and so structured rituals of disillusionment for young men and women to facilitate their transition into adulthood.

A classic example of ritually structured disillusionment from another culture may help to illustrate the place of disillusionment in the dynamics of the transition to adulthood.[1] The Hopi are a small tribe of indigenous North Americans, numbering no more than nine thousand people, who live in pueblos in Arizona and New Mexico. Religion is a central focus of Hopi life and culture. Hopi religious life revolves around the *kachinas,* who spend six months among the people and then six months in the spirit world. The *kachinas* are the spirits that bring all good things, including rain, food, and life. The term *kachina* refers to the spirits themselves, to the spirits present as the masked *kachina* dancers who are among the Hopi during six months of their liturgical year, and to the *kachina* dolls that are carved and given to children as part of their instruction in Hopi life. The Kachina Society is the largest and most important of the Hopi religious organizations. It is responsible for the ceremonies in which the *kachina* dancers take part.

Children are initiated into the Kachina Society (or another religious organization) as they enter adolescence, which for the Hopi is the beginning of adulthood. At the end of an elaborate three-day ritual, the children who are being initiated into the Kachina Society, along with their ceremonial parents, await the arrival of the *kachinas* (the masked dancers) in a *kiva*, a subterranean room used for religious purposes. The children are excited to be in the *kiva*, an adult space. They are excited to meet the *kachinas* for the first time in this special religious space. Their expectations are high.

The *kachinas* have danced during ceremonies all the children's lives, have brought the children gifts, have rewarded and punished the children's behavior during religious ceremonies, and are known to the children as the source of all good things. But this time, with the children waiting along with their ceremonial parents, the *kachina* dancers coming down the ladder into the *kiva* are *carrying their masks instead of wearing them*. This is a moment of intense disillusionment and shock for the children. They are confronted starkly with the reality that the *kachinas* who have danced for them in ceremonial festivals all their lives are also their brothers, fathers, uncles, and cousins.[2]

Interviews with Hopi adults about their experience of the initiation ritual reveal that they undergo a series of inner transformations begun by this shocking experience of disillusionment. First they are disoriented. They report feelings of anger and sadness. Then they become more interested in their religion. They report listening more carefully and perceptively to what the wise old ones teach them. (A period of special instruction by the elders begins after the ritual.) They take their religion more seriously. All this happens for them, however, only after they have had to confront and negotiate an experience of disillusionment that opens up for them powerfully the ambiguity and complexity of their own religious heritage and their own identity.

The experience of disillusionment that the initiates into the Kachina Society undergo begins a process of transformation. That process takes them from one way of being in the world and from one way of being related to their religious heritage to another. The world and the self they knew is undone, and space is opened for the growth of adult selves with a deeper and more profound appreciation of their religious tradition's teachings and practices. The initiates are changed utterly through this process of transformation. They think, feel, and act differently. They *are* different; they cannot go back to being who they were before.[3]

Demographic, cultural, religious, economic, and other factors make the situations of women in Christian churches vastly different from those of Hopi adolescents being initiated into the Kachina Society. The greater heterogeneity of our culture leaves us room to try out a wide range of responses to experiences of disillusionment with our religious heritage: from willed conformity, to persistent open rebellion, to disaffiliation from our tradition, and everything along the spectrum. Because of its focus on individualism, our culture and religious communities provide little if any guidance on how to interpret and negotiate the inner transformations that disillusionment initiates. To say the least, this makes it difficult for women to discern whether their experiences of disillusionment with the Christian religious heritage contain life-giving possibilities. Do our experiences of disillusionment with our religious tradition invite us to a deeper encounter with the reality that both grounds and transcends what we have learned Christianity to be and what we have thought our own identities to be? "Standing by a river, dying of thirst" powerfully symbolizes our situation and the possible invitation to renegotiate our relationship to our religious heritage that it contains. If the invitation rings true and we respond, it will change us. We will be different and our relationships to our world, our religious heritage, our community, and our way of being with God will be altered.

Longing, Voice, and Faith

Responding to the invitation contained in simultaneously hungering for God and being disillusioned by our religious heritage initiates a process that begins when we *listen to our longing*. Some women find this uncomfortable at first because it requires that we take ourselves and our lives seriously. Busily concerned about the needs of others, many women experience distress, even feel sinful, when they turn attention to themselves. But it is vitally important to listen to our longings; for life, for others, for God. We are called to take ourselves seriously, genuinely to cherish ourselves as precious in God's eyes. Listening to our longings is the first step. Our longings are a place of intimate connection with our God because they also reveal God's longing for us.

Learning the disciplines of listening to our longing—cherishing ourselves, paying attention to the thoughts and feelings that move within us, accepting feelings as feelings, enduring discomfort, refraining from hiding from our experiences of longing, discriminating between prior judgments and biases and the potential meanings in our life at this moment—all are important. These disciplines help a woman to acknowledge and move through the various responses she may have to her awakened longing: self-questioning, anger, confusion. They help her avoid the dismissal, denial, and numbing of these responses that are encouraged by the patriarchal world in which women live. The disciplines protect us from trying to escape the experience of frustrated longing by seeking safety through a willed conformity to some authority's version of Christianity or by locking ourselves into a stance of outright rebellion beyond the point where it is helpful to our own psychological and spiritual development. Learning to listen to our longings moves us naturally onto the path of creative engagement—with our experience and with our religious heritage. We begin to develop our awareness of ourselves and to understand ourselves. Developing the honest, gentle, discerning attentiveness that listening to our longings requires puts us on the journey to voice, the journey toward wise faith.

Learning to listen to our longings creates the possibility of renegotiating our relationship to our religious heritage. This listening strengthens a woman's sense of self, increases her trust in her own thinking and feeling. A woman who listens to her longings is compelled to begin to speak. She begins to find her voice. Often this happens for a woman when she begins to learn about her foremothers in faith and sees the resonances between their experience and her own.

A woman begins to renegotiate her relationship with her religious tradition when she undertakes the journey to voice. The journey to voice is a journey into faith for women. Once a woman finds her voice, she cannot relate to her Christian heritage, church community, or institutional religious leaders as she has before. She comes to understand how profoundly human and fallible her religious tradition is, especially as taught and practiced by her community. She also comes to understand, however, that her religious tradition is not defined by the constellation of teaching, practice, and institutional structures of her day or any given historical period. The Christian tradition is much richer, more ambiguous, surprising, and subversive. It carries wisdom that gives life in a community of earthen vessels. If all of this makes for less clarity and precision in a woman's faith, it also makes for a more realistic and alive faith.

Conceiving women's faith journeys as journeys to voice provides a ground from which to honor, criticize, and draw upon both our own lived experience and our religious heritage. It provides a zone of freedom, a space of altered perception and imagination that allows us to draw on the resources of our tradition even as we cope with the oppression of our patriarchal church.

Voice, Faith, and Wisdom

The journey to voice and faith, when traveled with integrity, leads us to a different way of being and perceiving and acting in the world. What once seemed only pain and frustration, "standing by a river, dying of thirst," now offers possibility of new life, not a quick and cheap new life, but a deepened and tempered one that expands the range of freedom of action and of imagination. Now a woman trusts her own experience, feeling, and thinking more. She can affirm that her pain and her resistance to oppression are faithful. She can test her own experience and thinking in the stories of her foremothers in faith. She comes to know as she travels the journey to voice and faith with integrity that women are called to be full selves, to live and not just exist.

The journey to voice and faith points to more discriminating perceptions about our inner lives, about our experience as human beings, and about how and where God is present in both. This approach to God, not through the resources mediated by office, the institutional priesthood, but through a discerning reading of the very stuff of our daily lives, leads women to their heritage in a new and more complex way. We come to appreciate that criticizing the Christian heritage does not put us outside the community, despite what those in power say. We affirm the authority of our own and our sisters' experiences of God. We come to appreciate how central discernment is to mature faith. Facing our experiences of oppression in the church, we become more sensitive to noticing and cooperating with the forces of God's Spirit working in the world.

When we appropriate our religious heritage in this different way we may experience our tradition's power to liberate, renew, and nurture in new ways. Now we relate to our religious heritage from a stance of discernment—noticing and cooperating with God's Spirit working in world and church—and not from a stance of self-denigrating submission—letting external institutional authorities define and interpret our inner lives. This different way retrieves and develops the constant but often unaccented theme in the Christian tradition's understanding of God and God's presence among us, the theme of Wisdom. Here is a place where the tradition may offer nurture and not destruction. Here is a place where the dissonance that we as women live in relation to our religious heritage is transformed into nurture for our spirits and armor against the destructiveness of an abusive institution. Here is a place that grounds our gifts and our full dignity in the community of faith, even when patriarchal leaders deny it. Here is the place that we come to understand Wisdom, not power or the authority of office, as the most trustworthy entrance to our religious heritage. We come to see how Wisdom is sometimes mediated through all of these and sometimes is not.

From the perspective of Wisdom, then, the conflicts over women's roles in the church, magisterial statements about women's ordination, institutional rules and regulations, are not to be understood automatically as divine directives. Wisdom is always suspicious of institutional authority because it sees it too often representing life for only part of a community. Institutional authority too often represents an order that is not perceiving the fullness of God's desires for humanity.

Wisdom's call to women in the church today is that we condemn the partialness and call the church back to Wisdom's more inclusive vision. Wisdom calls us to relate to our religious tradition in multiple ways. Directly addressing the institutional structures and leadership is important and the prophetic call of many courageous women in our midst is answering this challenge. Besides evoking prophetic confrontation, Wisdom also invites us to become more discerning about God's desires as these desires are recognizable in our individual and corporate lives, especially in the choices that we make. It invites us to hold institutional authority respectfully but lightly, accepting Wisdom's dictum that what brings life only for partial communities cannot finally be fully of God.

Wisdom offers us a sustenance that can motivate prophetic protest and constructive critique yet still savors God's presence and action loose in our personal lives and in the world. Women who experience Wisdom's sustenance find their attention and energies less preoccupied with the rules and procedures of the church and more attuned to discerning and cooperating with the movement of God's Spirit in our midst.

If we take Wisdom's route, we must become far more discerning about ourselves and our worlds. Wisdom requires the development of voice and the nurturing of mature faith. It requires women to stand in their places, knowing them to be partial but still filled with wisdom the world needs to hear. It requires women to accept the courage to live fully, even now, in the flawed realities of our church and world.

The path of Wisdom requires much of us. We must learn discernment, the ability to perceive the impulses toward life and death in any given situation or action. Our sensibilities must be shaped over a period of time. Practicing reflection and self-criticism is part of this learning process. So too is noticing and even apprenticing ourselves to women in whom we perceive Wisdom.

Once we begin down the path of Wisdom we are confronted immediately with the inertia to change in ourselves, other individuals, communities, and institutions. There exists a tension between moving in the direction of life—which requires change; reframing of our experience; loss of objects, projects, or even people—and the desire to maintain stability and safety. Learning to negotiate this tension is another discipline we are called to practice along the path toward wise faith.

Qualities of Wise Persons

Why care about Wisdom? Whatever appeal this vision of life presented in Jewish and Christian Scriptures contains is matched by the challenges it presents to a woman's psychological and spiritual development. The path of Wisdom is not easy. Is this way of being in the world, a vision of human personhood rooted in ancient times, applicable for our own time? While each woman must finally answer this question for herself, recent attention given to wisdom by psychologists, anthropologists, and philosophers exploring the development and the destruction of individuals and societies at the end of the twentieth century suggests that this ancient theme may speak to us.

Researchers exploring wisdom focus on the qualities that wise persons manifest, their senses of themselves, their visions of purpose and meaning for themselves and for existence, and the ways they act in the world. The researcher' findings suggest a mode of human existence focused on creative, compassionate living.

Wise individuals exhibit a marked awareness of their own inner process. They notice and can identify the diverse feelings, impulses, imaginings, and desires that cluster in particular ways for them in any concrete situation. They are open to the full range of human emotions that any situation evokes in them. Their awareness leaves them remarkably free to be at peace and to act in creative ways.

I experienced this awareness in conversations with a former student who felt called to a ministry of pastoral care for victims of AIDS in a war-torn African country and who after eight years is still there. I felt it deeply in a colleague who chose quality over quantity of life in her struggle with cancer, and showed all whom she touched how to live till we die. These are women who know how to negotiate their inner lives.

Neither mesmerized, obsessed, nor deceived by their inner processes, wise persons have a capacity to be open to their lives, both the inner and outer dimensions. They do not deny experiences of loss or grief but demonstrate a marked comfort with their feelings without being caught in or defined by them. Etty Hillesum moved in this direction in *An Interrupted Life*, the diary she wrote before being shipped by cattle car to Auschwitz. We may encounter such wisdom in friends or parents who have suffered great loss and who are candid in conversation with us about what that experience is for them. Or we recognize it in persons whose courage and freedom to act for life against seemingly unsurmountable odds move us deeply, perhaps Mother Teresa of Calcutta, the martyr Ita Ford, or the mother of Harlem, Martha Hale.[4]

Wise individuals are discerning about their world and their relationships. When Dorothy Day, Lucy Burns, and other women marched for the vote and endured imprisonment, beatings, and forced-feedings to press their cause in the early part of the twentieth century, they knew that they would face violent opposition. They acted anyway. When Martin Luther King, Jr., composed his *Letter from the Birmingham Jail,* he addressed directly the self-deception of his white ministerial colleagues in the South and the North, their refusal to see how the gospel addressed racism in their midst. When a mother garners the courage to take on a school system to secure adequate services for her child with disabilities, she exhibits such discernment.

Above all else, wise persons discern deeper levels of reality and act in ways that lead to richer life for themselves and for other individuals, communities, and the planet. Their ability to do so arises from their capacity to discriminate between fleeting phenomena and more enduring truths and values. Wise individuals recognize that they are part of a larger context. They know that cultural, social, familial, and religious contexts have shaped and continue to shape their experiences and perceptions and the experiences and perceptions of others. Rather than chafe against the limits that are givens for us as enfleshed, enculturated beings, wise people embrace those limits, even while they hold them lightly and gently. At the same time, they also are deeply appreciative of individuality, their own and that of the people around them. They are not threatened by or fearful of difference.

While wise individuals recognize and appreciate the contextual and embodied nature of human existence, their awareness of its limited and partial quality does not leave them adrift. Instead, it seems to make them more passionate and focused in their commitments. Wise people are deeply rooted in values and visions about life and meaning. They are invested in particular relationships and projects, willing for these commitments to shape them as human beings. Yet, they also have a remarkable sense of proportion in valuing. Their commitments are not idols. They hold their visions and values gently and are capable of giving up their projects and their particular visions for the future when these become obstacles to authentic existence for themselves and for others. Wise individuals seem to be organized internally and interpersonally around the desire to live with people and the planet in life-giving ways.[5]

Capable of experiencing their experience without fear and rooted in values and visions focused on full life for all of creation, wise individuals act in the world in particular ways. Their behavior and choices suggest a profound integration of their own souls with their agency in the world. They see myriad connections among ideas, actions, and choices that others do not see or, for reasons of self-interest, choose to ignore. They are comfortable with and notice the play of both affect and cognition in themselves and in those around them. Most characteristically, wise people act toward others and the world in ways that restore harmonious relations among individuals, communities, and other elements of the world.[6]

Few human beings are wise all the time and about all dimensions of their lives. Those who follow the path of wisdom, however, gradually extend the range of wise perception and action in their lives. Embodied in their attitudes and actions, these people influence the world around them for life.

Wisdom in Our Lives

Wisdom is not a rare commodity, the possession of only a few specially talented people. Wisdom is a constellation of perceptions and capacities that all human beings, even those with severe physical, emotional, or cognitive limits can exemplify to some degree in their lives. It is not a status symbol like entrepreneurial accomplishment or athletic prowess. It cannot be marketed or sold. This may be why our market-oriented, consumerist society is confused about wisdom. Wisdom is not about possession or control, or achievement, or conquest. It is about perception, participation, sharing, equality, individuality, and self-transcending delight in the welfare and good of others. Wise people know sorrow and joy.

While Wisdom becomes elusive in the effort to define it, thoughtful reflection on our own lives shows up encounters with Wisdom. We meet Wisdom in others and in ourselves, sometimes in direct encounters, sometimes through watching or reading or hearing about the lives of others.

A question, observation, or comment that surprises us and invites us to see ourselves and a situation differently often signals Wisdom. When a teacher asks us if the project we have chosen for a class is one for which we have some passion, she is talking about choosing wisely. When a counselor or friend points out to us that we have, for yet another time in our lives, acted precipitously in a work situation in a way that is detrimental to our chosen career, she is asking us to notice a pattern in ourselves, something Wisdom does. When a friend inquires whether the new house we are talking about purchasing will satisfy our heart's desire, she is speaking wisely. Teachers, parents, friends, counselors, pastors, siblings, strangers—any and all at various times in our lives may have invited us to view and experience life differently. When these invitations surprise us and arouse life and energy in us, they and the people who bear them are Wisdom for us. From skewed to harmonious, from isolated to richly connected, from limited to larger—such movements are not our own accomplishment but come to us as surprising and heart-expanding gifts. They are not without their challenges, but are clearly so precious and valuable that when we glimpse them or see them in the lives of others, we know them worthy beyond price.

Because the interchanges that bring Wisdom into our lives move us so deeply and profoundly, we may not have reflected on the person who offered us the graced intervention or the dynamics of the interaction itself. The carriers of Wisdom are other human beings like ourselves. At the moment that they invite us to see life in a new way, they act as mentor and guide, as wise persons who suggest and teach based on their own accumulated knowledge and experience of living. They are wise because they know how to live. In their wisdom they are willing to speak the truth to us—about our behavior, our attitudes, the consequences of our actions, our choices—and speak that truth in a way that focuses us on ourselves, not on them or their desires.

These carriers of Wisdom do not cajole or coerce; they invite, and leave us free to respond to the invitation, to test out the accuracy of what they suggest.

The mode of invitation and freedom of response is essential for Wisdom to work. Even helpful insights, when offered heavily laced with the presenter's agenda, or when put forth touched with coercion or manipulation, do not offer us Wisdom. One sees this when a mother pushes her daughter in the direction of one college or university over another, one career over another, one possible spouse over another. Interchanges laced with the initiator's agenda and feelings evoke self-protection or confused emotions in us. They make it very difficult for us to think clearly and feel discriminatingly about our own lives. Invitation and freedom are crucial for nurturing Wisdom in each one of us. They are the modes of profound respect for our dignity as creatures made in the image of God and for the power of God's Spirit at work in creation.

The individual who carries Wisdom for us is not perfect or flawless. Parents, teachers, pastors, neighbors, friends, counselors, strangers—all are human beings, all are earthen vessels. Indeed, the offering of Wisdom may be as graced a moment for that person as it is for us when we receive it. What experiences of Wisdom hold up for us and for those who carry Wisdom for us are the moments and trajectories of life defined far more by capacities for self-transcending delight instead of fear, for creation instead of destruction, for love instead of hate, and for joy instead of selfishness. Wisdom presents these choices not just as pragmatic choices for our benefit, but as acts of affirmation about the fundamental structures of the universe. It says that when we live in wise ways we bring not only ourselves but our part of the world into congruence with the deepest reality that exists. Wisdom invites choice, respects human freedom, and wagers that human dignity and creativity will transform the death, destruction, and chaos that pervade history.

There are special people in the lives of each one of us who have been carriers of Wisdom. A trusted aunt, uncle, teacher, or neighbor might play this role. Often these are people who fascinate us, people who have a capacity for life, a freshness in the way they react to situations, a humor and energy, that we find ourselves attracted to. We are fascinated by these people because they act in spheres of their lives out of an essential freedom that breathes life toward all whom they encounter. We find ourselves wanting to know what they know, to be able to do as they do, not in cheap imitation but in our own original way. Such people invite us to move more deeply into the journey of faith, to come to know God with an intimacy that allows such graced freedom of perception and action in the world to be sustained and expanded in our lives too.

The carriers of Wisdom whom we encounter may frighten us at crucial moments in our lives. When their vision of life's meaning and purpose scares or confuses us, or seems to require more than we can possibly bear, we may find ourselves tempted to denigrate and diminish and by whatever means possible rationalize away what they offer. We criticize them and how they live. Such a response diminishes us and closes us to Wisdom. Responses of resentment and envy mark a world of conventional wisdom, not the alternative Wisdom that is of God.

We have carried Wisdom for others in our own lives. Wisdom was present in us when, motivated by an energy and freedom that may have surprised us, we listened openly to someone whose story wearied us, spoke the truth clearly to a situation without the crossed energy that generates anxiety in listeners, or cared for ourselves or others without resentment or anger, even when we did not feel like it.

Noticing such moments in our lives points up for us the important characteristics of Wisdom and its presence among us. When Wisdom is present we are invited to richer lives but are left free to choose. When Wisdom is present we may be startled by our resistance to judging ourselves or our choices. Wisdom withholds judgment because it knows that God's love is powerful, that the work of grace is never finished, and that any human being has only a partial perspective on events. Wisdom is not a tool to achieve our particular purpose or agenda in life. Wisdom is not something that we possess. We can dispose ourselves to be open to it, we can intend to develop our capacities to notice and carry it, but we cannot make it happen. Wisdom entails an exquisite sensitivity to the delicate and expansive relationality of existence. It takes joy in its contribution to rich and authentic life but has no need to claim totality and control of any situation. Finally, Wisdom comes as gift to those who do not despise their own lives, their finitude, their joys, their grief, their creativity, their darkness, and their light. Wisdom does not come to those who will not be human beings.

Wise Women in Christian History

The biblical and historical women whose stories are included in earlier chapters embodied dimensions of Wisdom in their lives. They were human beings with their own talents, limitations, longings, joys, and brokenness. Each one of them, however, exemplified qualities of wise persons, in their respective pursuits of healing, wholeness, justice, creativity, and care for others. Each one focused on fullness of life here and now, for themselves and for others. None of them deferred life to some happy time after death. They discerned and lived according to the call of God in the midst of the day-in and day-out of ordinary history. They embraced life and did not flee from it.

Elizabeth the Wonder-Worker lived a life of profound intimacy with God. That intimacy transcended the conventions of her day. Elizabeth drew on this resource to lead her community. It guided her as she negotiated the ambiguities of her religious and political contexts. Such intimacy with God comes to wisely discerning women.

Mary Magdalene embraced her aching desire for Jesus. Unafraid of the pain that was tearing her apart, she grieved in the garden of death. With desire as her compass, Mary recognized the Risen Lord when he called her by name. In the exchange of voices she came to know that Jesus' tomb had become the womb of the new creation. She was first in John's gospel to announce it. Unafraid of the pain in her life, she received Wisdom's gift of new possibility.

The woman who was bent over could let healing flow through her when Jesus offered it because she had never rejected her life, even with its infirmity. The spirit that had possessed her and drained her strength could not destroy her deepest self. When she encountered healing power, she said yes from the core of her being, and stood up straight. Hers was a Wisdom that could move, even along obstructed paths.

The woman with the hemorrhage knew that her healing was of more importance to God than the purity codes of her day. She gambled that the alternative Wisdom of Jesus was more powerful than the conventional wisdom of her society, braved the crowds, and touched the Anointed One of God. In that gamble she won not only healing but a voice that spoke powerfully from the center of the crowd. Wisdom says that healing more than compliance with rules offers rich and authentic life for individuals and communities. Wisdom is not mute or invisible.

Margaret Gaffney Haughery knew how not to despise neediness, knew how to let her own desire and loss expand her heart to love even more. She chose life for orphans, the unemployed, poor workers, victims of war. Margaret knew that Wisdom cannot abide a community where some have plenty and others are in want.

Lucy Burns worked for women's suffrage. She knew that denying women the vote created only a partial community in the United States. Beaten, imprisoned, and force-fed, Lucy was not silenced. In times of mass arrest when the women would be sent to separate cells in an effort to weaken their resolve, she was the one who called the roll, and kept calling until every woman responded.[7] Lucy knew what Wisdom teaches: a partial community is no community at all.

Each of these women, through her relationship to her own humanity, through her capacities to perceive dimensions and relational patterns in reality that others could not, through her deliberate actions aimed toward others and the world to restore harmonious relations and richer existence, embodied dimensions of Wisdom. All were wise women of faith.

Though each was unique and embodied Wisdom with distinctive accents, all these women shared a particular way of relating to their religious heritages. For each, their sense of God's presence, grace, and call was mediated through their sense of purpose, justice, meaning, and healing in their lives. These women were not defined by religious institutions. They were defined by their own experience with a graceful and living God, by their own unique sense of God's call, their particular gifts, and how to use those gifts in their particular circumstances. All these women had a vision of richer life for themselves and for those around them. Their visions led them to transcend and subvert the conventional understanding of God's ways of acting and of appropriate roles for women in their day. These women were in touch with levels of reality below the surface of society and daily life. They read their relationship with God through the fullness of their lives, not through the dictates of leaders of religious institutions.[8]

These women's stories suggest that a woman finds her voice, grows in faith, and moves toward Wisdom when she begins to own the dissonance between institutional expressions of her religious heritage and her own lived experience, with all its ambiguity and complexity, as a place where God's Wisdom may speak to her. As women grow in voice and in faith they come to relate to their religious traditions with a deep but suspicious respect, keenly aware of how quickly institutions promote partial visions. Loosed from the fetters of slavish adherence to institutional dictates or overwhelming worry about official teaching, women who grow in faith and voice come to experience their tradition differently. Now they know it as a rich resource of stories, teachings, images, rituals, practices, and communities capable of mediating God's love, nurture, and liberating power in a woman's life. Joining this new knowledge with what spurred them on the path toward wise faith— experiences of the tradition's teachings, images, rituals, practices, and communities that obstructed God's love, nurture, and liberating power in their lives—women are called to a different place in their faith.

"I'm standing by a river, dying of thirst," said the newcomer to the group on that rainy, dark, February night. Giving voice to her own experience of intense desire and heartbreaking disillusionment, the newcomer shaped an image that captures the experience of many women in Christian churches today. We cannot stay where we are without destroying our souls. We cannot become unaware of our simultaneous desire and disillusionment. We can make the choice for life by responding to the invitation contained in our desire: the invitation to journey toward voice and toward Wisdom. Such is the way of wise faith.

Pause for Reflection

1. "Negotiating experiences of disillusionment is part of the process of growing into mature adulthood." Think about this statement.

Does it ring true in your experience? Identify and describe experiences of disillusionment that, for all their pain and disappointment, led to important changes and growth in you.

2. Identify two women in your experience whom you consider wise. Describe the encounter with each that led you to notice her wisdom. Describe the characteristics of wisdom that you see in their lives.

3. The path of Wisdom calls us to take responsibility for our lives and our actions and to stop running away from that responsibility by believing that external, institutional authorities are in control and know what is best. What is appealing to you about this call? What is frightening about it?

4. Retrieve a time in your life when you acted on your own authority even when others did not understand or support you. What happened? How were you strengthened by this experience? What was challenging about it?

Notes

1. A Glimpse into Wise Faith

1. Throughout this book I speak about women and women's experiences. I have chosen this perspective because the book has grown out of talks, retreats, and seminars with women. That I focus on women's experiences does not mean that I consider women the only oppressed group in the church. I simply have chosen to write to and about women. Other authors have and will continue to address the oppression of the poor, persons of color, the laity, and other groups.

Male friends who have read the manuscript have pointed out that the experience I address—simultaneously hungering for God and being disillusioned with one's religious heritage—is true for men as well, though the dynamics of it are somewhat different for men. They should remember, however, that this book is not addressed to them and does not claim to be a treatment of the subject for all human beings.

2. On the early Christian community's use of Wisdom as a way to understand Jesus see Elisabeth Schüssler Fiorenza, *Miriam's Child, Sophia's Prophet: Critical Issues in Feminist Christology* (New York: Continuum, 1994), and Marcus Borg, *Meeting Jesus Again for the First Time* (San Francisco: Harper & Row, 1994), 96–118.

3. Kathleen M. O'Connor, *The Wisdom Literature* (Wilmington, Del.: Michael Glazier, 1988). The theme of wisdom is being used in creative and quite distinct ways by feminist theologians today. Two recent and significant works are: Elizabeth Johnson's *She Who Is: The Mystery of God in Feminist Theological Discourse* (New York: Crossroad, 1992), and Schüssler Fiorenza, *Miriam's Child, Sophia's Prophet.*

4. See Robert Sternberg, ed., *Wisdom: Its Nature, Origins, and Development* (New York: Cambridge University Press, 1992).

5. For an elaboration of the concept of zones of freedom, see Sharon D. Welch, *A Feminist Ethic of Risk* (Minneapolis: Fortress Press, 1990) and also her *Communities of Resistance and Solidarity* (Maryknoll, N.Y.: Orbis Books, 1985).

2. Promise, Perils, and Ambiguity

1. On Wisdom in Jewish Scriptures see Kathleen M. O'Connor, *The Wisdom Literature* (Wilmington, Del.: Michael Glazier, 1988); Roland E. Murphy, "Wisdom in the Old Testament," in *The Anchor Bible Dictionary*, ed. David Noel Freedman (New York: Doubleday, 1992), vol. 6, 920–31; James L. Crenshaw, *Old Testament Wisdom: An Introduction* (Atlanta: John Knox Press, 1981); Dianne Bergant, *What Are They Saying about Wisdom Literature?* (New York: Paulist Press, 1984); and Leo G. Perdue, *Wisdom and Creation: The Theology of Wisdom Literature* (Nashville: Abingdon Press, 1994). In Jewish Scriptures the Wisdom literature is known as the Writings. In the Christian Scriptures the Wisdom literature includes the books of Job, Psalms, Proverbs, Ecclesiastes, Song of Songs, Wisdom, and Sirach. The themes of Wisdom, however, are not limited to these writings alone. On Wisdom in the Christian Scriptures see Elisabeth Schüssler Fiorenza, *In Memory of Her* (New York: Crossroad, 1985).

2. Walter Brueggemann, *In Man We Trust: The Neglected Side of Biblical Faith* (Atlanta: John Knox, 1972), 17–18. See also Arthur E. Zannoni, "Five Disconcerting Theological Reflections from Old Testament Wisdom Literature," *St. Luke's Journal of Theology* 19 (September 1976): 286–98; and Elizabeth Johnson, *She Who Is: The Mystery of God in Feminist Theological Discourse* (New York: Crossroad, 1992).

3. Brueggemann, *In Man We Trust*, 14–15, 17.

4. Ibid., 17–18.

5. Ibid., 18–19.

6. Ibid., 19–25.

7. Marcus Borg, *Meeting Jesus Again for the First Time* (San Francisco: Harper & Row, 1994), 69–88, 96–118; see also Schüssler Fiorenza, *Miriam's Child, Sophia's Prophet: Critical Issues in Feminist Christology* (New York: Continuum, 1994), especially chaps. 1 and 5.

8. Borg, *Meeting Jesus Again for the First Time*, 75–80.

9. Ibid., 80–88.

10. Ibid., 74.

11. Ibid., 70–74.

12. On Jesus' presentation of God's love as "wombish," ibid., 47–48, 85; Maria Pilar Aquino, *Our Cry For Life: Feminist Theology from Latin America* (Maryknoll, N.Y.: Orbis Books, 1993), 130–38.

13. Borg, *Meeting Jesus Again for the First Time*, 80–88.

14. Rita Gross, "Androcentrism and Androgyny in the Methodology of History of Religions," in *Beyond Androcentrism: New Essays on Women*

and Religion, ed. Rita M. Gross (Missoula, Mont.: Scholars Press, 1977), 9–10.

15. See Gerda Lerner, *The Creation of Patriarchy* (New York: Oxford University Press, 1986).

16. Mary Jo Weaver, *New Catholic Women: A Contemporary Challenge to Traditional Religious Authority* (San Francisco: Harper & Row, 1985), 3.

17. Ibid., 1–3. Jay Dolan does a little better than Hennessey. See Jay Dolan, *The American Catholic Experience: A History from Colonial Times to the Present* (Garden City, N.Y.: Doubleday, 1985), and James Hennessey, *American Catholics: A History of the Roman Catholic Community in the United States* (New York: Oxford University Press, 1981).

18. See the essays in Karen Kennelly, ed., *American Catholic Women: A Historical Exploration* (New York: Macmillan, 1989); James Kenneally, *The History of American Catholic Women* (New York: Crossroad, 1990); and Jane Redmont, *Generous Lives: American Catholic Women Today* (New York: William Morrow, 1992).

19. For example, the physical and professional threats to women who participated in the Re-Imagining Conference and the dismissal of M. Carmel McEnroy, R.S.M., from her teaching position at St. Meinrad's Seminary. Re-imagining God, Community, and the Church was an ecumenical conference of feminist theologians held in Minneapolis in March 1993. Some women lost positions in denominational structures because of their participation. Women teaching in seminaries were threatened with sanctions. See "Reacting to Re-Imagining," *Atlanta Journal Constitution,* May 21, 1994, E6:1; "'Re-imagining' Foments Uproar among Presbyterians," *Washington Post,* June 4, 1994, C7:1; "Presbyterians Try to Resolve Long Dispute," *New York Times,* June 17, 1994, A24:1; "After 'Re-imagining' God, the Reality of Job Loss," *Washington Post,* July 2, 1994, B7:2; "Presbyterians Seek to Heal Internal Rift," *Houston Post,* July 3, 1994, A37:6. For the case of Sr. Carmel McEnroy, see "Bishops Want Feminist Professor Fired," *National Catholic Reporter,* March 31, 1995, 3, and "Meinrad Teacher Resigns to Protest Firing," *National Catholic Reporter,* May 26, 1995, 5.

20. For information on the situation of women in the United States and abroad, see *The World's Women 1995: Trends and Statistics* (New York: United Nations, 1995); Linda Schmittroth, ed., *Statistical Record of Women Worldwide* (Gale Research Publications, 1991); Cynthia M. Taeuber, ed. *Statistical Handbook of Women in America,* 2d ed. (Phoenix, Ariz.: Oryx Press, 1996); Timothy H. Fast and Cathy Carroll Fast, *The Women's Atlas of the United Sates,* rev. ed. (New York: Facts on File, 1995), especially 57–121 and 175–88.

21. Mary Catherine Bateson, *Composing a Life* (New York: Atlantic Monthly Press, 1989).

22. See Constance FitzGerald, O.C.D., "Impasse and Dark Night," in *Women's Spirituality: Resources for Christian Development,* ed. Joann Wolski Conn (New York: Paulist Press, 1986).

23. The story of Elizabeth the Wonder-Worker is taken from Eva Catafygiotu Topping, *Holy Mothers of Orthodoxy: Women and the Church* (Minneapolis, Minn.: Light and Life Publishing, 1987), 145–46. The interpretation of the story is my own.

24. Contemporary Christian women are suspicious of self-denial, and for good reason. It has been used to keep women alienated from themselves. But a practice that is inappropriate in one time because it cuts a woman off from herself can in another historical period be a liberating practice. When we consider Elizabeth and other foremothers in faith, it is important to see them within their own contexts. Carolyn Walker Bynum has opened well the world of medieval Christian women. See her *Fragmentation and Redemption: Essays on Gender and the Human Body in Medieval Religion* (New York: Zone Books, 1991) and *Holy Feast, Holy Fast: The Religious Significance of Food to Medieval Women* (Berkeley: University of California Press, 1987).

25. The phrase is most associated with feminist theologian Nelle Morton. See *The Journey Is Home* (Boston: Beacon Press, 1985).

3. Listening to Our Longings

1. After using the story of Mary Magdalene in a parish mission, Chris Ondrala brought to my attention the poem "Mary of Magdala, I" by Mary Lou Sleevi. The poem uses the image of fulcrum and world-changing encounter as well (see Mary Lou Sleevi, *Women of the Word* [Notre Dame, Ind.: Ave Maria Press, 1989], 69–72). I also want to note here that I am using Mary Magdalene's story and those of other biblical women later as evocative stories that disclose movements in the inner lives of women. *I am not using a strictly historical-critical* approach to these texts.

2. Longing is a theme that runs through scripture. Many of the psalms, for example, Psalms 13, 63, and 77, express longing. Longing is a central theme in spiritual theology as well, for example, in St. Teresa of Avila.

3. American Association of University Women, *The AAUW Report: How Schools Shortchange Girls* (Washington, D.C.: The AAUW Educational Foundation and National Education Association, 1992). See also Lynn Mikel Brown and Carol Gilligan, *Meeting at the Crossroads: Women's Psychology and Girls' Development* (Cambridge, Mass.: Harvard University Press,

1990); Dorothy Dinnerstein, *The Mermaid and the Minotaur: Sexual Arrangements and the Human Malaise* (New York: Harper Colophon Books, 1976); Susan Basow, *Gender Stereotypes: Traditions and Alternatives* Belmont, Calif.: Brooks/Cole, 1986). The messages little boys receive are becoming increasingly ambiguous. How this is influencing their capacity to desire, articulate goals, and achieve them is beyond the scope of this book.

4. See Harriet Goldhor Lerner, Ph.D., *The Dance of Anger: A Woman's Guide to Changing the Patterns of Intimate Relationships* (New York: Harper & Row, 1985); Jean Baker Miller, M.D., *Toward a New Psychology of Women* (Boston: Beacon Press, 1975). Fathers do this as well, to both sons and daughters.

5. See *American Women in the Nineties: Today's Critical Issues* (Boston: Northeastern University Press, 1993); Daphne Spain, *Balancing Act: Motherhood, Marriage, and Employment among American Women* (New York: Russell Sage Foundation, 1996); *Women's Issues* (New York: H. W. Wilson, 1993); Winnie Hazou, *The Social and Legal Status of Women: A Global Perspective* (New York: Praeger, 1990); and Patricia Ireland, *What Women Want* (New York: Dutton, 1996).

6. The historical literature on how women throughout the centuries of Christianity resisted men's efforts to deprive them of place and voice in the community of Christ is growing. Recently work on medieval Christian women has addressed this question most pointedly. See Richard Woods, O.P., "Medieval and Modern Women Mystics: The Evidential Character of Religious Experience," Occasional Paper, Alister Hardy Research Centre, Westminister College, Oxford, OX2 9AT, England; idem, "Women and Men in the Development of Late Medieval Mysticism," in *Meister Eckhart and the Beguine Mystics: Hadewijch of Brabant, Mechthild of Magdeburg, and Marguerite Porete*, ed. Bernard McGinn (New York: Continuum, 1994), 147–164; Caroline Walker Bynum, Steven Harrell, and Paula Richman, eds., *Gender and Religion: On the Complexity of Symbols* (Boston: Beacon Press, 1986); and Susan Dowell and Linda Hurcombe, *Dispossessed Daughters of Eve: Faith and Feminism* (London: SPCK, 1987).

7. This reflection includes sections from the reflection on the woman bent over in Patricia O'Connell Killen and John de Beer, *The Art of Theological Reflection* (New York: Crossroad, 1994), 91–94. Working from scripture, I am developing the woman's story.

8. The biographical information on Margaret Gaffney Haughery is taken from *Notable American Women 1607–1950: A Biographical Dictionary*, ed. Edward T. James (Cambridge: Belknap Press of Harvard University, 1971), 2:153–55.

4. Embracing Frustrated Longing:
A Woman's Act of Faith

1. These incidents between women and priests are not told to "bash" male clergy. They are simply stories that women have shared with me.

2. See Mary Jo Weaver, *New Catholic Women: A Contemporary Challenge to Traditional Religious Authority* (San Francisco: Harper & Row, 1985), 18–20; Barbara Sicherman, Carol Hurd Green, with Ilene Kantrov, Harriette Walker, *Notable American Women: The Modern Period: A Biographical Dictionary* (Cambridge, Mass.: Belknap Press of Harvard University Press, 1980), 124–25. I am aware that both my historical examples are Catholic women from the Irish heritage. I have chosen these women because they fit well the themes with which I am working and because I am familiar with them. Much more work needs to be done on Catholic women of all ethnic heritages before we can begin to assemble a picture of the full range of Catholic women's experiences of faith.

3. A few of the major works embodying this critique include: Elizabeth Clark and Herbert Richardson, eds., *Women and Religion: A Feminist Sourcebook of Christian Thought* (New York: Harper & Row, 1977); Mary Daly, *The Church and the Second Sex* (New York: Harper & Row, 1975); Carol Christ and Judith Plaskow, eds., *Womenspirit Rising: A Feminist Reader in Religion* (San Francisco: Harper & Row, 1979); Catherine Mowrey LaCugna, *Freeing Theology: The Essentials of Theology in a Feminist Perspective* (San Francisco: Harper & Row, 1993); Elisabeth Schüssler Fiorenza, *But She Said: Feminist Practices of Biblical Interpretation* (Boston: Beacon Press, 1990); Rosemary Radford Ruether, *Sexism and God-Talk* (Boston: Beacon Press, 1993); idem, *Gaia and God: An Ecofeminist Theology of Earth Healing* (San Francisco: Harper & Row, 1992); Anne Carr, *Transforming Grace: Christian Tradition and Women's Experience* (San Francisco: Harper & Row, 1988); Susan Cady, Marian Ronan, and Hall Taussig, *Wisdom's Feast: Sophia in Study and Celebration* (San Francisco: Harper & Row, 1988); Ada Maria Isasi-Diaz and Yolanda Tarango, *Hispanic Women, Prophetic Voice in the Church: Hispanic Women's Liberation Theology* (San Francisco: Harper & Row, 1988); Delores S. Williams, *Sisters in the Wilderness: The Challenge of Womanist God-Talk* (Maryknoll, N.Y.: Orbis Books, 1993); Mary Jo Weaver, *New Catholic Women: A Contemporary Challenge to Traditional Religious Authority* (Bloomington, Ind.: Indiana University Press, 1995); and Elizabeth Johnson, *She Who Is* (New York: Crossroad, 1992).

4. Robert K. Merton, *Social Theory and Social Structure* (New York: Free Press, 1968) identified ritualism, rebellion, and innovation as pos-

sible responses in a social system when the effective relation between goals and means becomes confused, producing "anomie." Willed conformity is like Merton's ritualism, outright rebellion like his rebellion, and the third option introduced later, creative engagement, moves in the direction of his innovation. Another useful approach to their anger for women in the church is discussed in Carolyn Osiek, *Beyond Anger: On Being a Feminist in the Church* (New York: Paulist Press, 1986).

5. The Power of Voice

1. See Evelyn Eaton Whitehead and James D. Whitehead, *Christian Life Patterns: The Psychological Challenges and Religious Invitations in Adult Life* (New York: Crossroad, 1992); and Alice Miller, *For Your Own Good: Hidden Cruelty in Child-Rearing and the Roots of Violence* (New York: Farrar, Straus, and Giroux, 1990). Learning to say "no" is an important part of our psychological, moral, and spiritual development.

2. For information on the situation of women in the United States and abroad, see *The World's Women 1995: Trends and Statistics* (New York: United Nations, 1995); Linda Schmittroth, ed., *Statistical Record of Women Worldwide* (Gale Research Publications, 1991); Cynthia M. Taeuber, ed. *Statistical Handbook of Women in America*, 2d ed. (Phoenix, Ariz.: Oryx Press, 1996); Timothy H. Fast and Cathy Carroll Fast, *The Women's Atlas of the United Sates*, rev. ed. (New York: Facts on File, 1995), especially 57–121 and 175–88.

3. Mary Field Belenky, Blythe McVicker Clinchy, Nancy Rule Goldberger, Jill Mattuck Tarule, *Women's Ways of Knowing: The Development of Self, Voice, and Mind* (New York: Basic Books, 1986), 18–19. Henceforth this text will be referred to as *WWK* and its authors as the *Women's Ways of Knowing* Collective.

4. Kathleen M. O'Connor, *The Wisdom Literature* (Wilmington, Del.: Michael Glazier, 1988) provides a good introduction to Wisdom. See also "Wisdom" in the *Interpreters Dictionary of the Bible* (Nashville: Abingdon Press, 1976); Walter Brueggemann, *In Man We Trust: The Neglected Side of Biblical Faith* (Atlanta: John Knox Press, 1972); and Elisabeth Schüssler Fiorenza, *Jesus: Miriam's Child, Sophia's Prophet* (New York: Continuum, 1994), chaps. 1 and 5.

5. Tillie Olsen, *Silences* (New York: Delta/Seymour Lawrence, 1978); idem, "I Stand Here Ironing," in *Tell Me a Riddle* (New York: Delta/Seymour Lawrence, 1961), 1–12. *Silences* also speaks to the issue for male writers as well.

6. Carol Gilligan, *In a Different Voice: Psychology Theory and Women's Development* (Cambridge: Harvard University Press, 1982).

7. *WWK*, 11–12, 17–18. See also Nancy Goldberger, Jill Tarule, Blyche Clinchy, Mary Belenky, *Knowledge, Difference, and Power: Essays Inspired by Women's Ways of Knowing* (New York: Basic Books, 1996).

8. *WWK*, 15.

9. See Ellyn Kaschak, *Engendered Lives: A New Psychology of Women's Experience* (New York: Basic Books, 1992).

10. Mary Catherine Bateson, *Composing a Life* (New York: Atlantic Monthly Press, 1989), 1–18, 232–41.

11. In this section I primarily rely for a theoretical base on the works of the *Women's Ways of Knowing* Collective, Gilligan, and Miller.

12. See Janice L. Doane, *From Klein to Kristeva: Psychoanalytic Feminism and the Search for the "Good Enough" Mother* (Ann Arbor: University of Michigan Press, 1992). I want to note here that what I am saying is true for boys as well, though in different ways. We also must recognize that because a girl's mother is so important in her development, she also can be the most damaging influence in her life.

13. See *WWK*, 23–34, on "voicelessness."

14. Barbara Fiand, *Wrestling with God: Religious Life in Search of Its Soul* (New York: Crossroad, 1996), quoting Christin Lore Weber, *Womanchrist: A New Vision of Feminist Spirituality* (San Francisco: Harper & Row, 1987).

15. See *WWK*, 35–51, on "received voice."

16. See *WWK*, 51–86, on "subjective knowledge."

17. See Belenky, 87–130, on "voice of reason."

18. See *WWK*, 130–52, on "integrated voice."

19. Besides *WWK*, see Charles Davis, *Body as Spirit: The Nature of Religious Feeling* (London: Hodder and Stoughton, 1976), 1–17.

20. The work of James Fowler on faith development provides another way to think through the material in this section. See his *Stages of Faith: The Psychology of Human Development and the Quest for Meaning* (San Francisco: Harper & Row, 1981); see also Sharon Parks, *The Critical Years: The Young Adult Search for a Faith to Live by* (San Francisco: Harper & Row, 1986).

21. See Robert A. Orsi, *Thank You, St. Jude: Women's Devotion to the Patron Saint of Hopeless Causes* (New Haven: Yale University Press, 1996).

22. Recent works on medieval Christian women are illustrative here. See Richard Woods, O.P., "Medieval and Modern Women Mystics: The Evidential Character of Religious Experience," Occasional Paper, Alister Hardy Research Centre, Westminister College, Oxford, OX2 9AT, England; idem, "Women and Men in the Development of Late Medieval Mysticism,"

in *Meister Eckhart and the Beguine Mystics: Hadewijch of Brabant, Mechthild of Magdeburg, and Marguerite Porete*, ed. Bernard McGinn (New York: Continuum, 1994), 147–164; Caroline Walker Bynum, Steven Harrell, and Paula Richman, eds., *Gender and Religion: On the Complexity of Symbols* (Boston: Beacon Press, 1986); and Susan Dowell and Linda Hurcombe, *Dispossessed Daughters of Eve: Faith and Feminism* (London: SPCK, 1987). See also Caroline Walker Bynum, *Fragmentation and Redemption: Essays on Gender and the Human Body in Medieval Religion* (New York: Zone Books, 1991). A quite different illustrative example is how African slaves in the United States drew on the resources of Christianity (see Albert J. Raboteau, *Slave Religion, the "Invisible Institution" in the Antebellum South* [New York: Oxford University Press, 1978]).

23. The term is from *Women's Ways of Knowing.*

24. See *Women's Ways of Knowing*; see also Emily Hancock, *The Girl Within* (New York: Fawcett Columbine, 1989).

25. See John Shea, *Stories of God: An Unauthorized Biography* (Chicago: Thomas More Press, 1978), 25–39; Peter Berger, *A Rumor of Angels: Modern Society and the Rediscovery of the Supernatural* (Garden City, N.Y.: Doubleday, 1970).

26. Anne Frank, *The Diary of a Young Girl: the Definitive Edition*, ed. Otto H. Frank and Merjam Pressler (New York: Doubleday, 1993); Etty Hillesum, *An Interrupted Life: The Diaries of Etty Hillesum, 1941–1943*, intro. J. G. Gaarlandt, trans. Arno Pomerons (New York: Pantheon Boos, 1983); Corrie Ten Boom, *The Hiding Place* (Uhrichsville, Ohio: Barbour and Company, 1983); Phyllis Zagano, *Ita Ford: Missionary Martyr* (New York: Paulist Press, 1996).

27. Plays and films provide ready examples here: *The Miracle Worker*, *Silkwood*, *St. Joan*, among others.

28. *WWK*, 18–20, 144–52.

29. See John Shea, *The Spirit Master* (Chicago: Thomas More Press, 1987), 31–41.

6. Finding a Voice, Discovering Faith: Becoming a Public Person

1. The freedom Jesus leaves to the woman here is critical. For contemporary women it is vital precisely because so many women do not distinguish between touch and the violation of their bodies and spirits that is the consequence of abuse.

2. I am using the translation of the Hannah's story and relying on the interpretation of it from John Petersen, "Plotting and Poetics in I Samuel 1," unpublished paper. Used with permission. On Hannah, see also Trevor Dennis, *Sarah Laughed: Women's Voices in the Old Testament* (Nashville: Abingdon Press, 1994), 115–39; and Marcia Falk, "Reflections on Hannah's Prayer," in *Out of the Garden: Women Writers on the Bible,* ed. Christina Buchmann and Celina Spiegel (New York: Fawcett Columbine, 1994), 94–102.

3. This pattern of behavior on Elkanah's part is androcentric. Even if his intention was well-meaning, he acted only with reference to his assessment of the situation. He defined Hannah's reality.

4. Petersen, "Plotting and Poetics," 1–8. For a different interpretation of Elkanah's questioning of Hannah, see Cynthia Ozick, "Hannah and Elkanah: Torah as the Matrix for Feminism," in Buchmann and Spiegel, *Out of the Garden,* 88–93. Ozick attributes positive intentionality and tone to Elkanah's questions.

5. Petersen, "Plotting and Poetics," 8–9. Both Falk and Ozick note that Hannah's prayer to God at the shrine was a breakthrough event because shrines were not places of personal prayer in the life of the Hebrew people at this time. This tradition will develop only later with the synagogue. Hannah invents personal prayer in public space. The significance of her crying out to God relates to her and to her people.

6. Note again the androcentric pattern of behavior on Eli's part.

7. Petersen, "Plotting and Poetics," 9–11.

8. Ibid., 11–12, 15–20.

9. See Walter Brueggemann, "The Exodus Narrative as Israel's Articulation of Faith Development," in *Hope Within History* (Atlanta: John Knox Press, 1987), 7–26; idem, "Covenanting as a Human Vocation: A Discussion of the Relation of the Bible and Pastoral Care," *Interpretation* 33 (April 1979): 115–29.

10. Brueggemann, "The Exodus Narrative," 10–16.

11. Ibid., 7–26, 18.

12. Ibid., 16–20.

13. See Falk, "Reflections on Hannah's Prayer."

14. Rene Girard's theories on the role of scapegoating in maintaining cultural and social order are relevant here. See his *Violence and the Sacred,* trans. Patrick Gregory (Baltimore: Johns Hopkins University Press, 1971).

15. Bruegemann, "The Exodus Narrative," 19.

16. Ibid., 25.

17. J. Cheryl Exum, *Fragmented Women: Feminist (Sub)version of Biblical Narratives* (Valley Forge, Penn.: Trinity Press International, 1993), 18–21.

See also Phyllis Trible, *Texts of Terror: Literary-Feminist Readings of Biblical Narratives* (Philadelphia: Fortress Press, 1984), chaps. 3 and 4.

18. An exegetical issue surrounding these texts concerns whether such women—these in particular—were historically real or figures in a story. For my purposes it makes little difference. Even to be able to imagine this happening to women suggests a world in which women were vulnerable in the extreme.

19. Ilana Pardes, *Countertraditions in the Bible: A Feminist Approach* (Cambridge, Mass.: Harvard University Press, 1992), 6–12. Another reading of Miriam here is that she was punished for saying the wrong thing. That would be a problem only if her voice was strong.

7. Voice as Faith: Women's Path

1. Maria Harris, *Dance of the Spirit: The Seven Steps of Women's Spirituality* (New York: Bantam Books, 1991).

2. Ibid., 1–19.

3. Ibid., 35–51.

4. Ibid., 183. On European preoccupation with witches, see Bengt Ankarloo and Gustav Henningsen, eds., *Early Modern European Witchcraft: Centres and Peripheries* (Oxford, England: Clarendon Press, 1990); and Anne Llewellyn Barstow, *Witchcraze: A New History of the European Witch Hunts* (San Francisco: Pandora, 1994). There were men among the witches burned, though a disproportion number of women were killed.

5. Harris, *Dance of the Spirit*, 182–85.

6. Ibid., 70–72.

7. Ibid., 187–89.

8. Ibid., 188–89.

9. Beverly Wildung Harrison, "The Power of Anger in the Work of Love," in *Weaving the Vision: New Patterns in Feminist Spirituality*, ed. Judith Plaskow and Carol P. Christ (San Francisco: Harper & Row, 1989), 220. See also Fran Ferder, "Zeal for Your House Consumes Me: Dealing with Anger As a Woman in the Church," in *Women in the Church I,* ed. Madonna Kolbenschlag (Washington, D.C.: Pastoral Press, 1987), 95–113.

10. Harris, *Dance of the Spirit,* 58–85; Brueggemann, "The Exodus Narrative," 20–24.

11. See, for example, Ann O'Hara Graff, ed., *In the Embrace of God: Feminist Approaches in Theological Anthropology* (Maryknoll, N.Y.: Orbis Books, 1995) and Mary Aquin O'Neill, "Toward a Renewed Anthropology," *Theological Studies* 36:4 (December 1975): 725–36.

12. Valerie Saiving, "The Human Situation: A Feminine View," *Journal of Religion* 40 (April 1960): 107.

13. Ibid., 104–7. This is a point of major feminist critique. See, for example, Harrison, "The Power of Anger in the Work of Love."

14. Anne Carr's work in theological anthropology is particularly helpful for understanding this point (see *Transforming Grace: Christian Tradition and Women's Experience* [San Francisco: Harper & Row, 1988], 117–33).

15. Saiving, "The Human Situation," 108–9.

16. See, for example, the essays in Joann Wolski Conn, ed., *Women's Spirituality: Resources for Christian Development* (New York: Paulist Press, 1986) and the constructive systematic theology of Elizabeth Johnson, *She Who Is: The Mystery of God in Feminist Theological Discourse* (New York: Crossroad, 1992).

8.   *Walking Wisdom's Path*

1. The description of the Hopi Kachina Society initiation ritual is taken from Sam D. Gill, *Native American Religious Action: A Performance Approach to Religion* (Columbia, S.C.: University of South Carolina Press, 1987) and Don C. Talayesva, *Sun Chief: The Autobiography of a Hopi Indian*, ed. Leo W. Simmons (New Haven: Yale University Press, 1942).

2. The closest example of this for Anglo culture in the United States may be when children discover who Santa Claus is, though Santa does not play as central a role in the lives of children or the larger society as do the *kachinas* in the lives of the Hopi.

3. The history of religions shows similar rituals built around disillusionment, beginning at least with the Elysian mysteries in ancient Greece. Only in the modern period in Western European and United States cultures has the significance of confronting and negotiating disillusionment to the development of religious maturity been downplayed. Vestiges of its importance are found in early versions of Grimm's fairy tales and in the works of Hans Christian Andersen. See Mircea Eliade, *The Sacred and the Profane: The Nature of Religion*, trans. Willard R. Trask (New York: Harcourt and Brace, 1959); idem, *Rites and Symbols of Initiation: The Mysteries of Birth and Rebirth*, trans. Willard R. Trask (New York: Harper & Row, 1965); Paul Ricoeur, *The Symbolism of Evil*, trans. Emerson Buchanan (New York: Harper & Row, 1967).

4. Etty Hillesum, *An Interrupted Life: The Diaries of Etty Hillesum, 1941–1943*, intro. J. G. Gaarlandt, trans. Arno Pomerons (New York: Pantheon

Books, 1983); Phyllis Zagano, *Ita Ford: Missionary Martyr* (New York: Paulist Press, 1996); Brian Lanker, "Clara McBride Hale," *I Dream A Word: Portraits of Black Women Who Changed America* (New York: Stewart, Tabori, and Chang, 1989), 54–55.

5. Robert Inchausti explores the ways that Wisdom works in the lives of ordinary people who have ended up being very public figures in the twentieth century. It is unfortunate that so few of his subjects are women (see *The Ignorant Perfection of Ordinary People* [Albany: State University of New York Press, 1991]).

6. For a summary of definitions and characteristics of wisdom, see James E. Birren and Laurel M. Fischer, "The Elements of Wisdom: Overview and Integration," in *Wisdom: Its Nature, Origins, and Development*, ed. Robert Sternberg (New York: Cambridge University Press, 1992), 317–32.

7. Inez Haynes Irwin, *Angels and Amazons: A Hundred Years of American Women* (Garden City, N.Y.: Doubleday, Doran Company, 1934), 354–55, 382–87.

8. Their approach makes these women the mothers of women today who write feminist theology, interpreting God from the perspective of women's experience.

OF RELATED INTEREST

---■---

Teresa McGee
THE COMFORTER
Stories of Loss and Rebirth
Ten vivid stories written from the heart of a
gifted storyteller—true stories about
unforgettable people who find a tenacity for life,
often amidst an ocean of pain.
0-8245-1567-6; $14.95

Margaret D. Minis
I DON'T MIND SUFFERING
AS LONG AS IT DOESN'T HURT
Margaret Minis has written a wry but comforting
reflection on "ordinary" life lived in the care of
God for all those who have ever had their life
plans edited by a Higher Power.
0-8245-1438-6; $10.95

---■---

*At your bookstore or, to order directly from the publisher,
please send check of money order (including $3.00 shipping
for the first book and $1.00 for each additional book) to:*

THE CROSSROAD PUBLISHING COMPANY
370 LEXINGTON AVENUE, NEW YORK, NY 10017

We hope you enjoyed Finding Our Voices. *Thank you
for reading it.*

crossroad